A PRAYER FOR HOPE

A PRAYER FOR HOPE

I Can't. You Can. I'm Yours.

Father David Scotchie

Uramado Press

A Prayer for Hope: I Can't. You Can. I'm Yours.

Contact:
Father David Scotchie
Nativity Catholic Church
3255 N. Ronald Reagan Blvd
Longwood, Florida 32750

frdavidscotchie@gmail.com

Find me on Facebook at: www.facebook.com/frdavidscotchie

Cover Art: Theresa Degler
Book and Cover Layout: Tim Schoenbachler
Father Scotchie Photo: Joe Genovesi

First Printing: September 2014
Second Edition: January 2021

DEDICATION

To my family, with all my love –

Dad & Mom

Larry and Karin, Sarah, Anna

Theresa and Brad, Erin and Danny, Matthew, Alyssa

Mike and Karen, Michaela

Dan and Wendy, Luke, Ben, James

Julie and Rob, Sailor, Lila

Table of Contents

Preface to the Second Edition

When people come to me with their struggles, I often give them a copy of *A Prayer for Hope*. The book offers a way to pray for hope better than I can explain in a brief conversation. The book gives them something to read and practice. Some have told me that they have adopted the prayer "I can't. You can. I'm yours," and found a new strength. A friend in a 12-step program gives the book to those he sponsors as part of their recovery from addiction. I am gratified that it is a means for spiritual growth and pastoral care for so many.

This second edition follows the reading-friendly format of my book *Can I Say a Prayer with You? A Beginner's Guide to Praying with Someone.* The size of the print is bigger. The margins are wider and the line spacing greater. The additional white space and larger headings make it easier to read. Every little bit helps!

Chapter One, "I Can't," has added a few thoughts about habits and their power. Habits automate our daily activity like brushing our teeth so that we can use our conscious thought to think about the day's plans. While willpower might succeed in one-time efforts, habits win the long game. They can be a reason why we are stuck at "I Can't." With sustained and supported effort, habits can be changed to become part of the way forward to a virtuous life.

Chapter Four, "Powerlessness Is An Opportunity to Pray," includes a new prayer exercise to help the reader pray where they are. We usually spend our time in prayer wishing we were in a better place. When we recognize where we are in our joys and hopes and griefs and sorrows, there we find the Lord. It is the best place to start when we are powerless. The chapter adds a section "Offer It Up" which reflects on how our suffering can join us in prayer with the suffering of Christ on the cross.

In response to readers' requests for questions they can use for group discussion, I have added discussion questions at the end of each chapter. The individual reader might well benefit from the discussion questions in their own reflection. The memory verse at the end of each chapter, in addition to the longer psalm, prayer, or hymn, recalls the ancient custom to commit scripture to memory. Chewing on scripture, like a cow with its cud, makes it part of one's being.

I considered dipping a toe into the question, "What can Christians hope for?" with explicit church teaching on Christian hope, its development from the early Church to today, and contemporary issues of hope. But as this second edition has already grown by one-third, I have instead added endnotes that direct towards further reading in scripture, the *Catechism of the Catholic Church,* encyclicals, and other references drawing upon church teaching on hope.

May these words open a way of hope!
Father David

Mary, Mother of God, 2021

Introduction

This prayer is for those who are in need of hope. If you are on top of the world and life has never been better, you have no need to read further. For those who have lost hope, this prayer is for you.

This prayer is for these people I have come to know through my twenty-seven years as a Catholic priest:

The woman who buried her husband and is starting her retirement alone.

The man given a second chance after ruining his first marriage, but daily walking the edge of his recovery.

The couple numb from infidelity.

The single mom working full-time and wanting a better life for her little girl.

The grandparents raising their grandson for their daughter who has mental health issues.

The many families, crushed by debt and shame and long-term unemployment, losing their homes.

The widow and widower who met and married to enjoy each other's companionship in their golden years, only he has early signs of Alzheimers.

The gay Catholic not knowing whether he is welcome in his own church.

Prayer is a refuge in difficult moments. When a day is going poorly, there is no better way to turn it around than prayer. This prayer is for more than a bad day. It's a prayer to be said by those in a bad way.

The prayer has only six words. Life is hard enough without something long and difficult to remember. Six words, though, can say much. The first three chapters talk about the prayer two words at a time. The fourth chapter explores how times of despair can become opportunities for grace. The fifth chapter shows some of the fruits of this prayer such as humility, gratitude, and discipleship.

There is reason for hope here.

Let's begin.

ONE

I CAN'T

I CAN'T STOP…

I love chocolate. Dark chocolate or milk chocolate, it does not matter to me. Chocolate mixed with almonds, crème-filled chocolates, and flavored chocolate such as mint or orange are God-given delights.

I would like to cut back on chocolate. I would not mind losing a few pounds. My doctor would be much happier if chocolate was not one of my major food groups. Chocolate does not live long in my pantry. I do not buy chocolate, but somehow chocolate finds me.

You might have your own daily arm-wrestle such as losing weight. You might resolve to eat only vegetables, fruits, and grains. After three days, you have given in to the craving for fast food. Somehow without even trying, you and your car are in the drive-through lane ordering a cheeseburger, large fries, and a soda.

Efforts at self-improvement seem to run the same course. Consider the man who signed up to take a class in Spanish. Speaking Spanish would help him at work and maybe help with a promotion. But as he worked the night shift, the Spanish class played havoc with his sleep schedule. He could not figure out how to fit in Spanish and sleep. In the end, he stopped going to the Spanish class. Not wanting to be seen as a quitter, he never told the teacher that he was dropping out. He just disappeared.

Efforts to correct bad habits suffer the same fate. "Quitting smoking," Mark Twain quipped, "is easy." He added, "I've done it a hundred times." Staying quit was his struggle. Yours might be with gambling. Before you realize it, an online gambling site has half of your week's pay. You have to borrow again to pay the rent.

Your struggle might be with your temper. You keep your cool at the office and hold your tongue at home. You have learned to count to ten, go for walks, and breathe through your nose. Despite it all, you blow up and say things to your family which you deeply regret. They only know that it has happened before and it will certainly happen again.

Your burden may be a health condition such as Parkinson's disease. Your golden years have turned to rust, each day a struggle to dress and get into your wheelchair without falling. Using the bathroom is a humiliation. Dreams of travel and grandchildren have been replaced by the hard reality of your failing body.

Life is full of struggle and failure. The book *Delivered* by Matt Fradd is a collection of real-life stories of people struggling with sexual addiction. The beginning of each person's story was invariably about their increasing use of pornography that the person was no longer able to stop.

One couple, Mark and Anne, met in college and quickly became friends. She saw a young man who had grown up attending Catholic grade school and high school. An Eagle Scout and a captain of the baseball team, he was a clean-cut guy. He saw a beautiful young woman who was a good student and played college sports. Her Catholic faith impressed him. When they began dating, Mark shared his struggles with lust and pornography. Anne, unsure of his past, was nevertheless impressed by his honesty.

A week before their wedding, Mark bought his last pornographic magazine, or so he thought. He was convinced that, once married, he could walk away from years of pornography and masturbation and become a man of integrity with a great marriage.

In their times of sexual intimacy, the fantasies and images of the past distracted him. The internet became a gateway to porn binges. He confessed to Anne when he had fallen and promised that it would never happen again. Yet he knew that it was just a matter of time until the next fall.

Anne was angry, afraid, lonely, confused, and bitter. Miserable in her pain, she began to scream and yell so that he would know how much he was hurting her. Their disconnection deepened.

In their second year of marriage, they became pregnant. Meanwhile, Mark started using the computer at work to view pornography and dating websites. Flirting with women at work, he fantasized about meeting another person. He told Anne that he was thinking of leaving her. A week later, she miscarried. Adding to his shame and guilt, Mark eventually recognized that the stress he put Anne through may have caused the miscarriage. Numb, hollow and empty, he was not able to mourn with Anne their loss.

Although they sought some help with marriage counselors, their misery grew. Anne, fearing that Mark would cheat on her, gave him an ultimatum. He had to get help or get out.

Mark did get help. He took steps to break free of lust and become the man of integrity that he had dreamed of. Anne, too, had to seek help to restore their marriage. The first step in their recovery was hitting bottom. Mark had to face the hard fact that he could not stop on his own.

How hard it is to stop doing something even as it wrecks all we hold dear. Resolutions rarely work. Beaten, we give up. We hit bottom and admit, "I can't."

THE POWER OF HABITS

My adult prayer life owes a debt to monks. After graduating from the university, I spent a month at a monastery in Rhode Island to discern if I was a monk. In two weeks' time, I knew that I was not a monk. They went to church five times a day! The kicker was when two of us monastic visitors took a free afternoon to go the movies. We walked down the dark aisle of the movie theater, genuflected, and took our seats. Thank goodness the darkened movie theater hid our force of habit.

My month-long monastic immersion gave me the habit of daily prayer. A day does not pass when I do not spend several periods of prayer, at least fifteen minutes each, to praise God and pray for others. I wish that everyone could take a month at a monastery to gain the habit of daily prayer. But what do you do if you do not have a free month to spend at a monastery?

Before the libraries closed for several months during the COVID-19 pandemic, I made a commando run to the shelves. One of the books on CDs that I dumped on a whim into my book bag was a book called *Good Habits, Bad Habits* by Wendy Wood, a professor of psychology.

Habits are what we do without thinking: brush our teeth, wash our hands, drive the car to work. They free us up to concentrate on what most requires conscious attention such as watching for anything unusual on the road.

Good Habits, Bad Habits surveys decades of research on how we form habits. One of my big takeaways is how puny our willpower is before the power of habits. Teeth-gritting white-knuckle willpower can prevail in one-time efforts such as counting to ten in a particular argument instead of blowing up. But for repeated behavior such as dealing with anger, habits win in the long run. Habits own the long game.

You know already that I have a terrible sweet tooth for chocolate. In truth, my mouth is full of sweet teeth. After lunch, I might sneak a chunk of sugar in the form of dried fruit. Dinner is not dinner unless there is some sort of dessert.

Knowing that sugar is empty calories and sabotages my immune system, I have tried numerous times to kick the sweet habit. I have cleansed my cupboards of cookies and jams. I have shopped carefully to avoid items listing high fructose corn syrup in the ingredients. (Resistance is futile. High fructose corn syrup is in nearly every processed food item.) When I visit parish families and join them for dinner, I ask in advance that we have for dessert a piece of fruit instead of a store-bought cheesecake. One Lent years ago, I gave up sugar. It was a heroic grace-filled forty-day effort. On Easter Sunday, however, the chocolate bunnies reasserted their dominance. Somehow the sweets like the tide rise again. My willpower is not enough. I admit that "I can't." What is wrong with me? Why can't I just say no?

Our brains are wired to respond to rewards, receive cues from our surroundings and peers, and seek another path when faced with too much resistance. To form the habit of daily prayer, for example, I needed much more than willpower. I needed a month's immersion in a monastery where everyone went to common prayer five times a day whether they felt like it or not. I needed cues from the church bells calling us to prayer, the communal expectation of participation, the ease to show up, the repetition, and the reward of running with "the herd", in addition to the desire to pray. Willpower and self-control were necessary but only a fraction of what was needed to get in the habit of daily prayer.

Smoking cigarettes is another example of how much more than willpower is needed to change a habit. The percentage of Americans smoking cigarettes has dropped in half from over 40% after World War II to less than 14% today. Knowing that smoking cigarettes causes cancer did not kick the habit. Millions of Americans did not wake up one day and dump their smokes because it was no longer cool.

The decline in smoking has been correlated to many intentional changes apart from individual willpower. Laws banned smoking in restaurants, bars, airplanes, and trains. Taxes have helped triple the price of cigarettes in the past twenty years. We made it harder to get cigarettes when we took them out of vending machines and put them behind the store's check-out counter. Regulations scrubbed tobacco ads from TV and radio. As smoking was made more inconvenient, expensive, unpopular, and invisible, millions kicked the habit.

Even with these interventions, not every smoker can readily quit. According to the Centers for Disease Control and Prevention, more than half of adult cigarette smokers in 2018 made a quit attempt. Only seven out of one hundred of them succeeded. Meanwhile, 480,000 Americans die every year from cigarette smoking, and thirty times more live with a serious smoking-related illness. Smoking in the United States costs more than $300 billion a year in direct medical care and lost productivity.

Malcom X said that it was easier to quit heroin than to quit smoking. We know that nicotine is highly addictive. From the glass half-full perspective, the amazing thing is that millions have actually quit smoking. Habits, even the habit of smoking, can change.

There is an article that summarizes parts of the *Good Habits, Bad Habits*. https://www.newyorker.com/magazine/2019/10/28/can-brain-science-help-us-break-bad-habits. Dr. Wood has a website about her research on habits http://goodhabitsbadhabits.org/. No doubt there are countless books and programs that make use of good research to help us form good habits and reset bad ones.

All of this talk about habits is not separate from faith and morals. In fact, we have a church word for habits – virtue! The *Catechism of the Catholic Church* teaches, "a virtue is an habitual and firm disposition to do the good." What's more, "The goal of a virtuous life is to become like God."[1] Wow!

The virtue of temperance, for example, is the attitude that drives good habits for moderation and balance. Our typical day is like balancing on a unicycle. The unicycle requires constant motion rocking back and forth, pedaling forward and pedaling backward, all while keep one's arms extended like a balancing pole. We try to balance time with our families, a responsibility to care for elderly parents, and demands at work. Diet and exercise are another balancing act. We know we should eat better, but fast food is fast and convenient. Regular exercise is easier said than done – a walk once a week is not enough when thirty minutes of daily sweat is the recommended minimum – but there does not seem to be enough hours in the day.

The virtue of temperance is the virtue that gets us off the unicycle and leads us to a balanced day. "For Thomas Aquinas, temperance is the virtue that disposes us to proper balance, moderation, and due measure in realizing our desires," my former teacher at St. Meinrad Seminary, Father Mark O'Keefe, wrote in his book, *Virtues Abounding.*[2]

Temperance in eating – the habitual disposition to eat the right foods at the appropriate time in the right amount – is easier said than done. I love to eat. I love breakfast, snacks, lunch, snacks, dinner, and more snacks. Thomas Aquinas would rightly say that my lack of moderation in eating is the vice of gluttony. An ancient remedy for gluttony is fasting. No wonder that fasting on Ash Wednesday and Good Friday is a struggle!

Temperance in drinking – moderation in drink and in appropriate circumstances – is woven into Scripture. "Wine drunk at the proper time and in moderation is rejoicing of heart and gladness of soul" (Sirach 31:27-28). Or as Benjamin Franklin said, "Wine is proof that God loves us and loves to see us happy." Drinking to excess, on the other hand, opens the door to poor judgment and great suffering such as drunk driving.

Temperance in sex – the habitual disposition to act moderately and appropriately in the use of our sexuality – is also known as chastity. As God created sexual desire, it is in itself good and natural. Sexual activity in marriage is good as is its pleasure. The opposite of chastity is the vice of lust. Like gluttony, lust is a capital sin. It leads to other sins that corrupt and kill our relationships with the Lord and one another.

In our society, temperance in eating, drinking, and sex is up to the individual. In its view, you can eat, drink, and have sex as you desire. In contrast, being Christian means not indulging every desire. The Christian life cultivates instead the virtue of temperance to discern moderation and balance ordered not towards following one's passing desires but towards following Christ, who is our deepest desire.

Knowing about habits and virtues is good. Having resolve to form good habits and pursue virtue is great. Yet we still struggle. What started out as a slip can become a full-on face-plant fall when our appetites for food, drink, and sexual pleasure become immoderate. Our struggle might be with an abiding anger, a desire to get ahead and be held in high regard, or an appetite for nice things that comfort us and telegraph our value to envy of others. In short, our own efforts fall short. We come to a point and time when we admit, "I can't."

PRAY WHERE YOU ARE

A Buddhist monk, a Catholic priest, and a Protestant minister sat in their regular corner booth of the diner. During this monthly lunch, they were discussing the best position for prayer.

"The lotus position," the Buddhist monk explained, "is the best position for prayer. Sit cross-legged on the ground. Beginners may sit on a pillow. Legs crossed, you are stable and solid. Straighten your back. Rest your hands on your thighs and close your eyes. In this position, you are one with the earth. You can breathe easily. You can pray."

The Catholic priest shook his head. "Kneeling is the best position for prayer." He knelt next to the table to demonstrate. "Beginners may use a padded cushion or kneeler. Fold your hands and look up towards the crucifix. The position of kneeling signifies both humility and adoration before God. You pray best when kneeling."

"The Bible is the word of God," the Protestant minister began. "The best position for prayer is sitting with your Bible on your lap. Read the Bible. Let the Lord teach you. Sitting down is definitely the best position for prayer."

The waitress who was clearing their plates interrupted. "Excuse me, I could not help overhearing your conversation." She stepped forward. "In my experience, the best position for prayer was running out the door of the restaurant to get help for a grease fire that flashed from the griddle. That's when I prayed the best." The waitress picked up their plates.

Pray where you are. Sitting, standing, kneeling, or running out the door, the best prayer begins where you are. What sort of waitress escaping a kitchen fire would wait until she could fold into a lotus, kneel, or sit to pray?

Faced with an addiction, poor health, or a miserable relationship that has you whipped, that is where you pray. The prayer for when you are in need of hope begins with two words, "I can't."

We do not like praying, "I can't." It is painful. We do not like admitting despair. We want to move on. We want everything to get better. In our minds, we play down the seriousness of the moment. We might be caught up in wishful thinking that all will be well. "I can't imagine it getting any worse," we reason, "so it must get better."

Whether it gets better depends not on your starting point, but on whether you can honestly accept where you are starting.

My phone has a map application which I had rarely used. Having lived in the same parish for almost seven years, I knew all the streets. Someone could tell me that they lived on Salinger Road, and I could picture Salinger Road in the south part of the Avalon Park subdivision. I could tell you without looking at a map, "Drive down Mailer Boulevard about one mile, over a couple of speed humps. Turn right after the stop sign, and there is Salinger."

When I moved to my new assignment in a new parish, I was lost. I was familiar with the major roads, but once I turned onto a side street, I could drive and drive and still not find the house that I wanted to visit. I needed help.

The map application on my phone came in handy. I learned to type in the address of a parishioner. Within moments, the map on my phone marked their house with a red balloon.

As colorful as the red balloon marker was, it did not help me much. Yes, the red balloon showed me where the parishioner lived; but I still had to figure out how to get to their home.

Then I discovered that the map application could draw a route. The route was simply a blue line from where I was to where I wanted to go. All that was needed was my location.

To draw a route to my destination, the map application had to know where I was. Once it had my location marked with a blue dot, the map application would suggest several routes to the parishioner's house and estimate the travel time. After I picked one of the routes, the map application would draw a blue line down the highways and streets to the parishioner's house. As I began to travel, its electronic voice became my navigator, telling me, "Turn left in a quarter mile," and "Turn left now."

With little effort, I could find my way around my new town as if I had lived there for years. Two things were required: knowing where I wanted to go and knowing where I was starting from.

You know where you want to go. Get out of a bad relationship, get out of debt, find a job, restore a friendship, renew your marriage, become free of an addiction, resolve a crisis. Knowing where you want to go is half of the solution.

The other part is just as important. To draw a line from here to there, you first need to know where here is.

Start where you are. Name your current location. Accept that despite your best efforts, you are stuck.

In the situation where you are in need of hope, the starting point on your map is your powerlessness to make the situation better. "I can't" sums up what is going on. Like a blue dot on a digital map, "I can't" is your starting point.

YES, YOU CAN?

Our culture has convinced us, "Yes, you can!" With exclamation points and enthusiasm, our culture preaches, "There is nothing you cannot do! Confidence can change the world! All that you need is the right attitude!!!"

In a scene from the movie *Star Wars: Episode V - The Empire Strikes Back*, Luke Skywalker trained to become a Jedi Knight. He wanted to learn the ways of the Force.

As a Jedi Knight, he could defeat Darth Vader and help the rebellion overthrow the evil empire. With all his heart, he wanted to become a Jedi Knight.

To learn to become a Jedi Knight, Luke had a Jedi Master. Yoda, with his big pointed ears and wrinkled green brow, hardly looked like a Jedi Master. He leaned hard on his cane. Yet no taller than Luke's knee, Yoda trained Luke mercilessly.

In one scene, Yoda took Luke to the swamp where Luke had crashed-landed his space jet. The jet, sunken into the black oozing waters, was lost. Yoda pointed a knobby green finger at the swamp. "Use the Force to lift the sunken jet from the swamp."

Luke protested. "The jet is too heavy, the water too deep. It's impossible!"

Yoda sighed deeply and shook his head. "Always with you what cannot be done." Yoda looked up, disappointed. "Hear you nothing that I say? You must unlearn what you have learned."

Luke looked at the swamp and looked back at Yoda. Turning towards the swamp, he shrugged, "All right, I'll give it a try."

Yoda barked back. "No! Try not." Luke turned to him and Yoda drove home the lesson. "Do. Or do not. There is no try."

For the generations who have grown up with *Star Wars*, nothing could be plainer. Do or do not. It's simply a matter of attitude. Yes, you can. You only need to make up your mind.

Even as children we are taught that we can do whatever we make up our minds to do. *The Little Engine That Could* is an illustrated children's book first published in 1930. For decades, parents have read to their children the story of the little railroad engine that could.

One morning, as the story goes, a long train of freight cars asked a large engine in the roundhouse to take it over the hill. "I can't; that is too much a pull for me," protests the great engine though built for hard work.

The train asks another engine, and another, only to hear excuses and be refused. In desperation, the train finally asks the little switch engine to draw it up the grade and down the other side.

The Little Engine took the job. "I think I can," puffed the little locomotive. It hitched itself to the front of the long heavy freight train. Slowly the brave Little Engine built up speed, puffing faster and faster, "I think I can, I think I can, I think I can." Finally the Little Engine neared the top of the steep grade, which had discouraged the more powerful engines. Going slowly but still forward, the Little Engine puffed, "I – think – I – can, I – think – I – can."

The train reached the top of the hill. As the Little Engine pulled the train down the grade, it said in triumph, "I thought I could! I thought I could!" With positive thinking, the Little Engine had risen to the occasion and saved the day.

The story teaches a lesson that even a child can understand. Having learned it on our mother's knee, we have taken the can-do spirit to the heart of our cultural values. No wonder a 2007 poll named the *The Little Engine That Could*, "Teachers' Top 100 Books for Children."

We wallpaper our office cubicles with posters of Rocky figures hustling up stadium steps crowned with captions of the word "Persistence." A poster of a rock-climber hanging on a cliff sends the message that guts and tenacity will bring you to the top. A poster of a black steed frozen in a gallop amidst the blur of the field is crowned by one word – "Ambition." Inspiration and motivation surround us.

One author allowed that we are all going to get our share of lumps and bumps. The same life that brings the joy of father-daughter dances and the crush of dry crunchy leaves on the sidewalk will stab holes in our hearts. Those holes might be your husband leaving you, your headaches more serious than you thought, or your dog hit by a car. Life has its struggles.

The author advises that we face a choice: give in to gloom and doom or choose to grieve and move on. When life deals a blow, he encourages us to choose to move forward. The author concludes that we have the power to choose a life that is rich, satisfying, and truly awesome.

As proof of the value of the can-do spirit, he himself turned around his divorce and job loss with the gospel of positive attitude. From the ashes he raised up not one but two bestsellers and a multimillion-hit website.

The evidence is an avalanche. Our movies, children's books, and internet sing the same song, "Yes, you can!" People make a living telling others, "Yes, you can! Put your mind to it and you can accomplish anything!"

But what if you put your mind to it and still fail?

What If You Really Can't?

Losing hope in such an enthusiastic and positive world is doubly dooming. You already feel the weight of despair. Failing, despite your best efforts to change your attitude and put your mind to the task, adds to the shame. Your misery is compounded. Failure is not an option in a can-do culture. Who can you talk to about your downward spiral? Everyone else seems to have their life in order. It is easy to believe that there must be something wrong with you.

A positive attitude is commendable. Positive beats negative every time. Let me be clear that to pray "I can't" is not defeatist. It's not giving up or throwing in the towel. It is the third way. Between fight or flight, between trying harder or collapsing into despair, there is a third way. (I will say more about this in Chapter Four.) The third way is for those who have tried Yoda's way and failed. First, it starts with owning the truth and praying from your powerlessness. "I can't."

For Discussion

- "Teeth-gritting white-knuckle willpower can prevail in one-time efforts such as counting to ten in a particular argument instead of blowing up. But for repeated behavior such as dealing with anger, habits win in the long run." When has your willpower triumphed? When has it failed?
- "In the situation where you are in need of hope, the starting point on your map is your powerlessness to make the situation better." What is your blue dot starting point?

Memory Verse

"Show me the path I should walk,
for I entrust my life to you."
Psalm 143:8b

Psalm 143: *Lord, Hear My Prayer*

LORD, hear my prayer;
in your faithfulness listen to my pleading;
answer me in your righteousness.
Do not enter into judgment with your servant;
before you no one can be just.
The enemy has pursued my soul;
he has crushed my life to the ground.
He has made me dwell in darkness
like those long dead.
My spirit is faint within me;
my heart despairs.
I remember the days of old;
I ponder all your deeds;
the works of your hands I recall.
I stretch out my hands toward you,
my soul to you like a parched land.
Hasten to answer me, LORD;
for my spirit fails me.
Do not hide your face from me,
lest I become like those descending to the pit.
In the morning let me hear of your mercy,
for in you I trust.
Show me the path I should walk,
for I entrust my life to you.
Rescue me, LORD, from my foes,
for I seek refuge in you.
Teach me to do your will,
for you are my God.
May your kind spirit guide me
on ground that is level.
For your name's sake, LORD, give me life;
in your righteousness lead my soul out of distress.
In your mercy put an end to my foes;
all those who are oppressing my soul,
for I am your servant.

TWO

You (Lord) Can

You can.

These two words in the middle of this six-word prayer are spoken to God. After crying to heaven, "I can't," "You can" acknowledges that where we can't, the Lord can.

Well, then, what can the Lord do?

The Lord Can Change Lives

You may find it easy to give credit to God for Creation. From the Book of Genesis onwards, the Bible is clear that God made everything from nothing. He made the stars of heaven, the fish in the sea, and the birds of the air. The beauty of nature is awe-inspiring. A perfectly normal response is, "Wow!" The work of his hands surrounds you.

The power of God goes beyond Creation. He fashions new creations. The lives of the saints buoy confidence that God can recreate new lives here and now. He has made countless saints from rough wood. "You can" recalls that the Lord can change lives. Let's look at two Biblical saints to see what God can do.

When Jesus was crucified and buried in the tomb, all hope was buried with him. His followers had believed that he was the promised Savior. After all, Jesus had told them that he was the Son of Man. He had healed lepers, the blind, and the lame. He had fed five thousand with a few loaves and fishes. He had taught the multitudes about the reign of God. Jesus was the answer to their prayers.

His crucifixion changed everything. How could the Savior be crucified like a common criminal? How could God let his Chosen One come to such an end? The followers of Jesus were afraid that the authorities would come after them. Locking themselves behind closed doors, they went into hiding.

Then something happened – something really big happened. Fifty days after the public execution of Jesus, his followers hit the streets, no longer afraid. Peter, their leader, showed the way. This was the Peter who had hotly sworn three times during the trial of Jesus that he did not know him. Yet fifty days later, Peter stood up in the midst of a great crowd and made a shocking speech. In so many words he said, "Jesus was sent by God. You killed him and let a murderer go free. God raised him up. We are witnesses. We have seen him alive."

These were not the words of a frightened fisherman. They were the words of a fearless apostle. No longer afraid for his life, Peter and the other disciples wanted to tell everyone about Jesus Christ.

Some in the crowd became angry. Others were cut to the heart. "What should we do?" they asked. Peter told them, "Say you're sorry. Turn from your evil ways and turn toward the living Lord." On that day the Church was born. About three thousand persons, according to the Acts of the Apostles, were baptized that first Pentecost (Acts 2:14-41).

Peter's conversion was nothing short of a miracle. Through him, the Lord established his Church. But the Lord was not done changing lives.

As the Jesus movement grew in numbers, the authorities became worried. They sent a top man to deal with it. Saul was a zealous Jew. He had devoted his life to the study of the law of God and he fully followed the teachings of Moses.

Determined to stop the Jesus cult, Saul stood nearby and approved when the mob stoned Stephen, a follower of the Way of Jesus, to death. Saul went house to house and kicked down doors looking for Jesus followers, dragging men and women out of their homes and throwing them into prison. He traveled as far as Damascus to arrest any followers of the Way and bring them back to Jerusalem in chains.

Only, something happened along the road to Damascus. A light flashed from the sky. Saul fell to the ground. He heard a voice saying, "Saul, Saul, why are you persecuting me?" Saul did not know who was speaking to him. "Who are you, sir?" The reply came, "I am Jesus, whom you are persecuting. Now get up and go into the city and you will be told what you must do" (Acts 9:1-6).

Blinded by the light, Saul was led to Damascus. There, he was baptized and his name changed from Saul to Paul. The former persecutor learned everything he could about Jesus. He re-read the Scriptures in the light of his new faith. He took to the road. No longer arresting Christians, he was instead making Christians. He preached that not only the Jews could follow Jesus. Anyone, even Gentiles, could be saved through Jesus.

What can God do? He can change a person like Saul into Saint Paul. He can change Simon into Saint Peter. Gathering his scattered followers under the leadership of Peter, he can create a Church. That's what God can do.

If God can change Peter, a frightened fisherman, into the rock foundation of the Church and if God can change Saul, the mortal enemy of the Church, into its greatest champion, what can God not do?

There is a story of a peasant family immigrating at the turn of the century from the Old Country to New York City. Just off the boat, the mother and daughter looked for a store to buy food. The father and his boy wandered into the lobby of a skyscraper. There they saw a hunchback old woman dressed in black, propped up on a cane, looking at a wall.

Suddenly the wall silently opened. The old woman stepped into the wall. From either side, like barn doors, the wall closed upon her. Small bubbles of light appeared on the wall illuminating numbers. The bubbles went from the number one up to the number thirty. After a minute or two, the light bubbles reversed direction. From right to left, the numbers counted down.

When the light bubble with the number one was lit, the wall silently opened. A tall blond woman stepped out of the wall into the lobby. Dressed in a gray business skirt suit, she was more than easy on the eyes. She turned to the right and vanished into the street.

The immigrant father could hardly believe this wonderful new land of America. He turned open-mouthed to his son. "Boy, go get your mother!"

Wouldn't it be wonderful if we changed as magically as stepping into an elevator? Wouldn't it be a blessing if the Lord changed our lives with the push of a button?

The stories of the conversions of Peter and Paul suggest that the Lord changes lives as fast as a lightning bolt from the heavens. While above all else the Lord wants us to become full of his life and love, he usually leads us in small, less dramatic steps. Slowly and surely, the Lord does change lives, and more.

The Lord Can and He Cares

It is one thing to believe that God changed the lives of Peter and Paul. It is another thing, however, to believe that God would do it for you. The Lord is a God who can. Is the Lord a God who cares?

One of the most tender passages in the Bible is the Book of Isaiah, chapter 43. Through the prophet Isaiah, the Lord spoke to the Israelites. "Fear not!" the Lord called out, "for I have redeemed you." The Lord claimed the people as his own. "You are mine."

These words were spoken when the people of Israel were in exile in Babylon. Six hundred years before the birth of Christ, the Babylonian Empire conquered the tiny Kingdom of Judah and force-marched the captured Israelites to Babylon. For two generations, the people of the Promised Land were captive in a foreign land. With no hope of escape, they suffered their exile in slavery.

The Israelites understood their exile in Babylon to be a punishment for their sins. They had been unjust to the widow, orphan, and stranger. They had been unfaithful to God. The Babylonian exile was proof to them that God had let them suffer the consequences of their wickedness. They were on their own.

"You are mine." The words of the Lord broke through their darkness like the dawn. With these words from Isaiah, the Lord made clear that the people did not belong to the Babylonians. They did not belong even to themselves. The Lord claimed them as his own. The covenant still held. "I am your God; you are my people."

Whom was the Lord claiming as his own? The Israelite people had been defeated and deported. As slaves, they were an insignificant tribe well on their way to disappearing from history. The superpowers of Babylon and Egypt with their armies and chariots were far more worthy of the Holy One of Israel.

But the Lord did not see it that way. In fact, "I give Egypt as your ransom, Ethiopia and Seba in return for you." The most powerful nations on earth were not what the Lord wanted. He wanted Israel. He gave the strong in return for the weak. It was as if God made a deal to swap the wedding china for broken pottery. Why did the Lord make such a seemingly bad bargain?

"Because you are precious in my eyes and honored." Slaves in the eyes of the Babylonians, the Israelites were dishonored losers on the battlefield. Their cities had been sacked, their temple had been leveled. Yet in the eyes of the Lord, they were precious. His people were worthy of honor.

The Lord said bluntly, "Because I love you." The Lord loved them. Whether they loved themselves or not, it did not matter. It is as if the Lord was blinded by love. Leveling mountains and filling in valleys to make a smooth, straight highway, he brought his lovely people home. Why? "Because you are precious in my eyes and honored, and I love you."

What more needs to be said? With these tender words, the Lord declared openly his passion for his people. His passion would lead him to do even more extreme deeds through his son, Jesus Christ. Not only could he do all things, he would do all things, "Because you are precious in my eyes and honored, and I love you" (Isaiah 43:4).

You can find in the Bible many other instances where the Lord God cares for his people beyond all reason. In Ezekiel 36:26-28, for example, the Lord promises that he will give them a new heart and place a new spirit within them. They shall once again flourish in the land that he gave to their ancestors. In Galatians 2:20, St. Paul declared, "I live by faith in the Son of God who has loved me and given himself up for me." He asserted that although we were sinners following our own desires, by grace we have been saved by God, "because of the great love he had for us" (Ephesians 2:4). In the end, the greatest evidence of God's love for us is his saving work through Jesus Christ.

The Lord Wants To Do Wonders For You

The stories in the Bible happened long ago. Understandably, you can write them off as relics from the past. You might reason that God is busy with important matters such as creation and salvation. The planet has billions of people. Who are you to presume that God has time for your personal crisis? You may wonder whether the God of the cosmos is intimately involved in your daily affairs. You may find yourself honestly asking, "Okay, Lord, I believe you can. I believe you care. I'm just not sure if my worries are worthy of your attention. After all, who am I to trouble you?"

Despite our doubts, God is intimately involved in our lives. His love for us is stronger than a mother's love for her children or a bridegroom for his beloved

(CCC 219). He so loved the world that he gave his only Son (John 3:16).

Let me give you two personal examples, one short and one long, of how much little things matter to God.

One Friday afternoon, I was called to visit a parishioner at the hospital. The work on my homily for Sunday was going slowly and needed more time than I had planned. Besides the homily preparation, I needed to prepare for other activities and appointments for the weekend. Going to the hospital was not in my schedule. "Lord," I prayed silently, "how can I do all this? There's not enough time in the day. Help!"

In a few minutes, the phone rang. My Saturday morning nine o'clock appointment canceled due to work. I hung up. The phone rang again. My Saturday morning ten o'clock appointment canceled for a funeral. I hung up. I began to wonder why I was suddenly so unpopular. The phone rang again. The Saturday afternoon two o'clock appointment had opted for a family outing. I hung up.

I could not believe it. My schedule had gone from overbooked to wide open. Working a miracle with my calendar, God had answered my prayer. He showed me that he does things for me and cares about me. No matter how trivial my overloaded schedule might seem, it mattered to the Lord. If I took care of his people, he would take care of me. Handed a wide-open schedule, I went to visit the parishioner in the hospital.

Let me give you another example of God's personal touch.

When I became the pastor of a new parish, I was no longer in a parish with another priest. I was on my own. Missing the company of another priest, I decided that it was time to get a dog.

Inspired by the list that my brother had made when he was looking for the ideal wife – good-looking, sense of humor, smart, Catholic, wants kids – I made my own list. My ideal dog would be neither too big nor too small. Considering the Florida sun, it would have short hair and not shed fur. It would like to run, play with children, and love people.

I took my list to prayer. "Lord," I prayed, "I want a dog. Here's my list. I would appreciate it if you could help me."

Soon enough, I got a phone call. Asking to speak with a priest, Marcia had some specific questions about the Catholic faith. I drove to Marcia's home. We visited in her living room while her Australian sheepdog, Gracie, sat by Marcia's side.

Marcia leaned on her dining room table, Bible open. She had been away from the Catholic Church for a while. Although she had not been coming to the Catholic Church, she had been active in several Bible studies and Protestant churches. She asked me about the Real Presence. She asked me about salvation. We talked about works and faith and Mary, the Mother of God.

After an hour or so, Marcia and Gracie thanked me for the visit. She said that she would keep thinking about these things. On my way out the door, she asked if there was anything she could do for me.

Marcia, I had learned in our conversation, just so happened to be a veterinarian. "As a matter of fact," I said, "I'd like to get a dog."

Marcia said, "I'll be in touch."

A week later, Marcia gave me a call. "Father," Marcia said, "I found you a dog. It's a Corgi."

"What's a Corgi?"

"It's the kind of dog that Queen Elizabeth has," Marcia replied.

I pictured an extra-large, tan-and-white, furry dachshund with pointed fox ears, short legs, about a foot high at the shoulder, weighing about thirty pounds. This was not the dog I was looking for.

"Sorry, Marcia, that's not what I have in mind."

"Okay, I'll keep looking."

Another week passed. Marcia called, "Father, I found you a dog. Let's go get it."

"What kind of dog is it?"

"It's a Beagle."

I groaned. A Beagle? Beagles are hounds. They live by their nose. Following a scent, they have been known to get lost in the woods. Their baying, while good for broadcasting that they have chased a raccoon up a tree, is not a welcome sound in a suburban neighborhood.

Their urine stinks. They eat everything and grow fat. A Beagle?

It was too late. In no time, Marcia picked me up. We went to the Orlando airport. The U.S. Department of Agriculture kept nearby a kennel of a couple dozen dogs. It rescued Beagles from the local dog pound and trained them to detect fruits and vegetables entering airports and ports.

One dog, Pippin, had washed out of the training. She had displayed the excellent agility needed to climb over luggage and stairs. Untroubled by strange noises and surroundings, she had passed the airport test with flying colors. She was a real people-lover and good with kids. About eight months old, she was housebroken. Quick to learn, she already knew how to sit and shake. In the physical exam, however, she showed the potential for hip dysplasia.

You see, Pippin was not a purebred beagle. She was a beagle-shepherd blend. Shepherds tend to have bad hips. The USDA, wanting their inspection dogs to have a long service life, had decided that it was not worth investing the training in Pippin. Marcia had heard from one of the USDA workers who visited her veterinarian clinic that they had a dog, Pippin, up for adoption.

We walked into the little reception area. Marcia and I waited on the plastic chairs like parents eager for the delivery of a baby. Several of the staff, all female and suspicious, came into the room. We chatted. They asked me many questions. Had I owned a dog before? Would I be with the dog during the day or would it be alone? How long had I lived in my current residence? Did my house have a fenced-in yard? Marcia vouched for me.

Finally, they brought Pippin into the room. The first thing she did was to chase her tail. We signed the papers. She was mine.

Mindful of the name of my parish where I had been assigned, St. Maximilian Kolbe, I changed her name. Pippin became Maxie. That summer, Marcia trained me and I trained Maxie. She learned not to run away. She learned to eat only her food and not to eat my food. I taught her to stay, wait at the door, and come when I called her.

Maxie was the dog I had been looking for. She was about forty pounds, neither too big nor too small. She had short hair. She did not shed. She rarely barked and never bayed. She loved to run after Frisbees and tennis balls. With the kids and parishioners who came to the rectory, she was great. She was so well-behaved and easy in temperament (except around other dogs, more on that later) that I could take her along when I visited parishioners in their homes.

In short, Maxie was the dog I had prayed for. More interesting is that, while the Lord knew my list, I had never fully shared my list with Marcia, the veterinarian. I had only told her that I was looking for a medium-sized dog. The rest was in the hands of the Lord.

Marcia, by the way, came back to the Catholic faith. In fact, she found her own calling. Comfortable in

Protestant circles, she explained the Catholic faith to Protestants. She showed how the Catholic faith was based on the Bible. She even brought members of her Protestant Bible study to the Catholic faith.

Every day Maxie was a living, breathing, tail-chasing reminder to me that God not only could, but God cares. God not only could do wonders for me, God wanted to do wonderful things for me. He was not too busy saving the universe to trouble with me. When I prayed, "You can," I firmly believed, "You care."

For Discussion

- "While above all else the Lord wants us to become full of his life and love, he usually leads us in small, less dramatic steps." The conversions of Saint Peter and Saint Paul had dramatic leaps. When have you had a dramatic leap in faith? When have you been led in small, less dramatic steps?

- "God is intimately involved in our lives. His love for us is stronger than a mother's love for her children or a bridegroom for his beloved." How has God been intimately involved in your life? What is his love like?

Memory Verse

"I live by faith in the Son of God
who has loved me
and given himself up for me."
(Galatians 2:20)

Psalm 16: *Keep Me Safe, O God*

Keep me safe, O God;
in you I take refuge.
I say to the LORD,
you are my Lord,
you are my only good.
As for the holy ones who are in the land,
they are noble,
in whom is all my delight.
They multiply their sorrows
who court other gods.
Blood libations to them I will not pour out,
nor will I take their names upon my lips.
LORD, my allotted portion and my cup,
you have made my destiny secure.
Pleasant places were measured out for me;
fair to me indeed is my inheritance.

II
I bless the LORD who counsels me;
even at night my heart exhorts me.
I keep the LORD always before me;
with him at my right hand, I shall never be shaken.
Therefore my heart is glad, my soul rejoices;
my body also dwells secure,
For you will not abandon my soul to Sheol,
nor let your devout one see the pit.
You will show me the path to life,
abounding joy in your presence,
the delights at your right hand forever.

THREE

I'm Yours

"LORD, SAVE ME!"

She had a disaster on her hands. Sewage was backing up into the shower. Gloria knew how to raise her four kids. She knew how to bathe, clean, feed, and play with her pre-school kids, but she had no idea what to do about the backed-up plumbing. Her husband was at work and no help. He told her to call the plumber.

"Help us!" Gloria begged the plumber through the phone. The plumber came that afternoon. Gloria was never so glad to see a plumber. While she kept the kids out of the way, he took a look at the mess in the shower. He went outside to clear the line between the house and the sewer. In thirty minutes, he had worked his magic. The family could use their toilets again.

Although Gloria had a terrible mess to clean up, she was deeply grateful. "Thank you, thank you, thank you," she said to the plumber. She gave him a bottle of cold water as a token of gratitude. She did not mind the two hundred dollar service charge. In this emergency, the cost was easy to bear.

In dire straits, a common prayer said loud and often is "Help me!" This is a good prayer. Circumstances have moved you from the belief that you can handle life on your own to the recognition that some things like a clogged sewer pipe are beyond your ability. You need help.

You are in good company when you call on the Lord for help. The psalms pray "Help me, Lord!" in ways too many to count: "When I call, answer me, O God of justice" (Psalm 4), "Lord, save my life" (Psalm 143), "I am yours; save me" (Psalm 119), "Lord, hear my voice!" (Psalm 130), and "Lord, I call to you for help" (Psalm 88).

You could do worse than cry out like Peter the apostle, "Lord, save me!" (Matthew 14:30). He and the disciples were far from shore in a boat battered by the waves. In the midst of the storm, they saw Jesus walking on the sea. Though they were terrified, Peter bravely called, "Lord, if it is you and not a ghost, command me to come to you on the water." The Lord said, "Come."

Peter climbed out of the boat to start walking on the water towards Jesus. Then he noticed the strong wind. Becoming afraid, he began to sink. "Lord, save me!" Like a lifeguard, Jesus reached out his hand and caught him. When they settled into the boat, the wind ceased.

Like Peter, we instinctively cry out when sinking, "Lord, save me!" We know that we are over our heads. We don't see a way out. The storm is drowning us. Who would not follow Peter's example and cry out, "Lord, save me!"?

There is a danger to the cry, "Help me, Lord!" The danger is this: it risks reducing God to a divine plumber. When the pipe bursts and you have no water for cooking, the toilet, the shower, or drinking, you call the plumber. You are grateful that he shows up the same day. You are grateful that he fixes the pipe and you are grateful as he goes out the door. But that's the end of your relationship with the plumber. It's nothing personal, but you hope never to see the plumber again. All you want is your plumbing to provide water and take away the waste.

The cry from the foxhole, "Help me!" can treat God as a divine plumber. You are grateful when the crisis ends. You thank God for his help; but in no time, you resume your normally scheduled life. Until the next crisis, the Lord is simply not on your radar. You keep him on speed dial next to 911 in case of emergency. His job is to bail you out of a jam. He is otherwise not part of your life any more than a plumber would be.

MORE THAN A PLUMBER

God wants to help you more than any divine plumber could. He wants to share with you his own blessed life. In good times and in bad, in sickness and in health, the Lord God wants to be with you and you to be with him. God has been this way from the beginning.

The Book of Exodus in the Old Testament of the Bible begins with Israelites settling in ancient Egypt and multiplying in number. The Egyptian pharoah, fearing the population boom of the foreign people, oppressed them and forced them to labor for the Egyptians. When the Israelites continued to grow in number, the king reduced them to cruel slavery and commanded that the Hebrew male infants should be killed. The Pharaoh wanted to keep the upper hand. The Israelites groaned under their bondage and cried out.

The Lord heard the people's cry and remembered the covenant he had made with Abraham. He sent Moses to Pharaoh. After a series of plagues capped with the destruction of the first-born of the Egyptians, Pharaoh let the people go. They followed Moses into the desert. When Pharaoh and his chariots chased them, Moses parted the Red Sea in order that the people could pass through. After the people were safe, the Red Sea collapsed and drowned the Egyptian army. The Hebrews were finally free of their slave masters.

They were not yet home and far from the Promised Land. In fits and starts, they followed Moses who brought them to Mt. Sinai, where the Lord dwelled. At Mt. Sinai, the Lord made a covenant with the people. The Lord God said to them,

"See what I did for you. I carried you on eagles' wings out of Egypt. I brought you to myself. Even though the entire world is mine, I have chosen you as a special people to me. You will be for me a kingdom of priests and a holy nation. I will be your God and you will be my people" (Exodus 19).

What the Lord told the Hebrews was that before they even knew the Lord, he was acting on their behalf. He had freed them from centuries of slavery in Egypt. He had fed them in the desert and kept them alive. He would lead them to the Promised Land where they could live in peace. Much more than a divine plumber, he wanted an enduring relationship of trust with the people.

The Lord did all of this for the Israelites unconditionally. At Mt. Sinai, he revealed his desire for them. He told them what he had done for them so far. He made promises of what he would do for them. All that the people had to decide was that they could do no worse with the Lord as their God than they had done on their own.

It was a no-brainer. If not for the Lord, they would still be slaves in Egypt. With the Lord, they had hope for a better life. They had the incredible offer of God's own life. All they had to do was to say, "Yes! We are your people, you are our God."

Religion is sometimes labeled as a system of rules. For example, "Do not steal; do not kill; honor your mother and father." What can be overlooked is that the rules follow from the relationship. Your relationship with the Lord is the heart of the matter. How you live it out – the rules – follows from the relationship. The rules of religion exist to protect the relationship with the Lord.

A banana has two parts, the skin and the fruit. No one eats the skin. Yet who would buy a banana without a skin? Without a skin, the banana fruit quickly becomes mush. It spoils and smells, not even good for banana bread. The skin protects and preserves the fruit.

In the same way, the rules of religion protect and preserve the relationship with the Lord. As the purpose of the banana skin is to protect and preserve the fruit, the purpose of the rules of religion is a flourishing relationship with the Lord. Yes, there are rules. Yes, there are better ways and worse ways to live your relationship with the Lord. But the living heart (the banana!) is your relationship with the Lord.

The core rules became known as the Ten Commandments. But only after the Lord revealed to the Hebrew people his desire for them and only after he told them that he was the One who had brought them out of slavery did he set forth the rules. The rules followed from the relationship.

Beginning with, "I am the Lord your God, you shall have no other gods before me," a living relationship with the Lord meant a new way of life. In other words, the people had to decide to put their relationship with the Lord first. Before any other relationship or activity, including family, work, health, wealth, status, and reputation, the Lord was to come first.

Living out their new relationship meant a new way of living in order that the relationship with the Lord would grow and flourish. The new way of living meant for example "you shall not kill" and "you shall not commit adultery."

"I'm yours." These last two words of our six-word prayer for hope renew your relationship with the Lord. In biblical language, it is an act of covenant. Just as the Lord worked wonders for the Israelites even before they knew that it was his hand which had set them free, the Lord has been at work setting you free.

The response of the Israelites was to put their relationship with the Lord first. Similarly, "I'm yours" puts everything back into perspective. The all-important relationship with the Lord is placed front and center. Recalling the bond he has made with his people, you can say, "I'm yours. No matter what has happened or what will happen, I trust you."

I PLEDGE ALLEGIANCE

Ignatius was a soldier seeking glory. He found himself, in May of 1521, facing surrender or death. The Spaniards were defending the fortress of the town of Pamplona against the French, who claimed the territory as their own against Spain. As the Spaniards were few and the French were many, the Spanish commander wanted to surrender. Ignatius convinced him to fight on, if not for victory, then for the honor of Spain. Unfortunately, a cannon ball crashed into Ignatius. One leg was wounded and the other leg broken. The victorious French soldiers admired his courage. Rather than take him to prison, the French brought him to his castle of Loyola where he could heal.

The doctors had to break his leg to reset it. Ignatius endured the procedure without anesthesia. Despite their efforts, he did not heal but grew worse. He was told to prepare for death. Yet death was not ready for Ignatius and he recovered. Although his leg healed, the bone protruded below the knee. Ignatius could not imagine life without the long, tight-fitting boots and hose of the courtier. He had the doctors re-break and reset his leg. Once again, he endured the procedure without anesthesia. When he finally healed, one leg remained shorter than the other. For the remainder of his life Ignatius walked with a limp.

The long recuperation was boring. Unable to find any romance novels to pass the time, Ignatius read the only two books available, a book on the life of Christ and a book on the saints. To his surprise, the more he read, the more he considered the saints worth imitating. He dreamed of emulating their exploits in fasting, pilgrimages, and penance.

Ignatius noticed that after reading and thinking of the saints and Christ he felt peace and joy. Meanwhile, after thinking of a certain noble lady whose love he imagined winning, he felt restless and unsatisfied. This was the beginning of his understanding of discernment. God was using his feelings to lead him to a new way of life.

By the time he had recovered from his wounds and could travel, he had made up his mind. Putting aside his old desires of romance and worldly conquests, Ignatius still wanted glory. Only it would not be glory for himself. He would become a soldier for Christ and take as his motto, "For the greater glory of God."

He went to the Benedictine shrine of Our Lady of Montserrat. There he made a general confession in writing. Following the code of chivalry, he knelt all night in vigil before Our Lady's altar. He gave his allegiance to his new king, Jesus Christ. After he left his sword and knife at the altar, he gave away all his fine clothes to a poor man and dressed in rough clothes with sandals and a staff. His old life was over. His new life, thanks to a leg-shattering cannonball, had begun.

Ignatius went on to found the Society of Jesus. Better known as the Jesuits, it is a fellowship of men dedicated to the greater glory of God. Inspired by the spirituality of Ignatius, the Jesuits have established countless missions, universities, and schools. They have changed the course of the history of the church. Innumerable lives have been changed because Ignatius gave himself to the Lord.

Ignatius changed from a self-serving soldier to a Christ-centered saint. He changed from reading romance novels to writing a prayer that begins, "Take, Lord, and receive all my liberty." The prayer, known as the Suscipe, is at the end of this chapter. Suscipe is the Latin word for 'receive.' Ignatius asked the Lord to receive him that he might belong fully to the Lord. His life was dedicated to the pledge, "I'm yours."

THE LORD WANTS TO BE WITH YOU AND YOU WITH HIM

While in college, Valerie attended a Festival of Praise at the Franciscan University of Steubenville. She closed her eyes as people laid hands over her in prayer.

Eyes closed, she saw an image of Jesus flooding her with love. Bright, warm rays of white and red light were shooting from the heart of Jesus right through her. She felt kind and loving eyes pierce her soul. A tiny taste of heaven, his love was more intense, more powerful, and more real than any love from anyone she had ever known. From that day, Valerie knew the love of the Lord.

Years later, this time as a chaperone for a youth trip to another Steubenville conference, Valerie went to confession. For her penance, the priest sent her to the chapel to say, "Thank you, Jesus, for always loving me."

She took her strange penance to the conference chapel. As the chapel had no chairs, she sat on the floor. When she looked up, she was stunned to see a painting of the same image of Jesus that had appeared to her when she had been slain in the Spirit. The words "Jesus, I Trust in You" were written on the bottom of the painting.

Valerie felt overwhelmed in the presence of this image of Jesus. She began to say to him her penance, "Thank you, Jesus, for always loving me." She could not say it more than a few times before she was flooded with tears, joy, love, and mercy from the Lord.

Henry Nouwen wrote in his little book, *The Return of the Prodigal Son*, "The question is not 'How am I to love God?' but 'How am I to let myself be loved by God?'" Valerie, from an alcoholic family, struggled with self-esteem and anxiety. Her unspoken fear had been, "Do I believe that God simply wants to be with me?" Seeing the Lord's love melted her fear. The fear gave way to the desire to love the Lord.

Valerie later learned that the image of Jesus clothed in a white garment, his right hand raised in blessing and his left hand over his heart, from where two large rays came forth, one red and the other white, is how the Lord had appeared to Sister Maria Faustina Kowalska in a vision in 1931.

Sister Faustina asked the Lord about the meaning of the rays. In her diary she wrote the response she received. "The two rays denote Blood and Water. The pale ray stands for the Water which makes souls righteous. The red ray stands for the Blood which is the life of souls. These two rays issued forth from the depths of my tender mercy when my agonized heart was opened by a lance on the Cross. Happy is the one who will dwell in their shelter, for the just hand of God shall not lay hold of him."[3]

This image of Jesus revealed to Saint Faustina became known as the Divine Mercy. The message of Jesus to Saint Faustina echoed the message of the Gospel through the ages. God is a God of mercy. He has given himself to us completely and invites us to give ourselves to him.

Beyond any doubt, Valerie came to know the Lord. She not only knew God's love for her, she knew his mercy. She could say with her whole heart, "Jesus, I trust in you." Saying those words renewed and strengthened her trust in the Lord.

In the same way, when you pray "I'm yours," you renew and strengthen your trust in the Lord. Before any call to the Lord for help, before any promise you might make to follow his way of life, the Lord desires to share his own life with you. What can one say except, "I'm yours"?

Like Valerie, I have had my own experience of the Lord that has made it second nature for me to say to the Lord, "I'm yours."

I had been on a thirty-day silent retreat. During the retreat, my spiritual director asked me to take to prayer the story of the Prodigal Son.

At first, I wondered what more I could learn from this story. I knew that it was in Chapter Fifteen of the Gospel of Luke. I had memorized the story of the Prodigal Son. I had preached it numerous times at penance liturgies, told it to school children in the parish school, and had reflected on it with adults preparing for baptism at the Easter Vigil.

I knew how the younger son had returned home with his tail between his legs after he had wasted his share of the family fortune. Before leaving home, he had wished his father was dead. The most that he had hoped from his shameful return was a roof over his head and something to eat.

Like so many, I loved how the father ran to greet his younger son. He embraced and kissed him. Ignoring the son's lame words of sorrow, he commanded his servants to action. "Quick, put a ring on his finger and shoes on his feet. Clothe him in the finest robe. Slaughter the fattened calf. We are going to have a party. Let's celebrate! My son was lost, but now he is found. He was dead but now he has come alive again."

Instead of humiliating his son, the father gave his younger son the place of honor in his home. All that the son had to do was to show up.

The meaning of the story was obvious. Like the father, God welcomes us home unconditionally. He sent Jesus to restore the relationship between us sinners and God the Father. His message was not condemnation but reconciliation.

With this happy ending, you might think that the story is over. But that is not where Jesus ends the story of the prodigal son. The story continues.

The older son, on his return from his work in the fields, heard the music from the party. When he discovered that the party was for his wayward younger brother, he became so angry that he refused to enter the house. The father left the party and went outside to his son.

The older son let him have it. "I've slaved for you. I've never asked anything from you. I did everything you asked me to do. Without complaint, I took up the slack when your other son took off to waste the family fortune and disgrace the family honor with his wild living. Now he comes home and gets a party. It's not fair."

The father did not respond to anything the older son had said. He simply opened his arms and said, "All that I have is yours. You are so dear to me. But your brother has come home. He was dead and has come back to life. He was lost and now is found. Please, come inside and celebrate." The story ends with the older son and father standing outside the house.

That's where I found myself. As I prayed over the story in my imagination, the story took a turn. I found myself in the story standing outside a house lit up with an evening party. I saw the father embrace me. He put his arms around me without saying a word. I felt great love. I felt peace. If I could put his embrace into words, it was something like this:

"I love you, David. I love you, no matter what you have done or have not done. I do not care if you are a priest or anything else. You do not have to earn my love. I love you because I love you. And nothing you can do can change that."

It rocked my world. In that prayer I realized that all God wanted was to be with me and for me to be with him. How I lived and what I did was simply a way to live out that communion. I did not know what to do next.

In prayer, the Father made it clear to me. "If you want to stay outside, I will stay with you. I want above all else to be with you. But I would really like it if you came inside to join the party."

That's what I've been doing ever since. I've been closer than ever to the Lord. I have gladly joined his party. The words "I'm yours" sums up the acceptance of God's desire to be with me and for me to be with him.

Saying "I'm yours" is saying much more than "Help me, Lord!" "I'm yours" accepts that the Lord is your heavenly Father. Yes, he is at your side when the plumbing explodes. He is at your side because he never left you. He wants more than anything else in the world to be with you and for you to be with him. He wants you to be with him at his joyful party. "I'm yours" accepts his invitation, "Come inside and join the party!"

For Discussion

- Read the Book of Exodus, chapter 19. How does the covenant at Mt. Sinai change the people? Can you think of another covenant God has made with his people?

- Pledging allegiance to the Lord, St. Ignatius of Loyola took as his motto, "For the greater glory of God." How was this motto a change from his former way of life? What might be your motto that captures a change from a former way of life?

- You can use your body to say our prayer for hope. While saying, "I can't", put your hand on your heart. While saying, "You can", extend your arm to heaven. Put your hand again on your heart for "I'm" and extend your arm again to heaven for "yours."

- Spend some time with the image of the Divine Mercy, preferably in the presence of the Blessed Sacrament in a church. Pray the words, "Jesus, I trust in you." What do you notice?

- Read the story of the Prodigal Son in the gospel of Luke, chapter 15. Imagine yourself in the story. What does the Father do?

Memory Verse

"I am yours; save me"
(Psalm 119:94)

SUSCIPE:
Take, Lord, and Receive All My Liberty

Take, Lord, and receive all my liberty,
my memory, my understanding
and my entire will,
All I have and call my own.

You have given all to me.
To you, Lord, I return it.

Everything is yours; do with it what you will.
Give me only your love and your grace.

That is enough for me.

– St. Ignatius of Loyola

FOUR

Powerlessness Is An Opportunity to Pray

FIGHT, FLIGHT, OR…?

My dog Maxie can fool you. A medium weight beagle-shepherd mix, she is a kid magnet. Children swarm around her. "She's so cute!" they coo. Playing to the audience, she chases her tail and jumps from person to person to smell for treats. Looking up at you with her big doe eyes, she lets you scratch her behind the ears. She has not met a person that she does not like nor has she met a person who does not like her. Maxie gets all the attention a dog could want.

In the face of a threat, however, Maxie becomes a different dog. While she is a people lover, she has yet to meet a dog that she likes. Being a rescue, maybe she had had a bad experience in the pound. She walks with her tail up like a periscope, all alpha dog. On a walk with me that comes across another dog, her hackles stiffen. She pulls on the leash towards the other dog. She sniffs the other dog suspiciously. After a few seconds, something in her dog brain tells her that the sidewalk is not big enough for two dogs. Growling, she will lunge against her leash to dominate the other dog, no matter how big or small.

The scenario is the opposite when the other dog makes the first move. A foot-size terrier yapping as if it were the meanest Doberman in the junk yard will cause Maxie to move to the other side of the road and pick up the pace.

Once when I was visiting Maxie's vet, Marcia, at her home, her Australian sheepdog Gracie thought that Maxie needed to know who was top dog. As neat as a surgeon, Gracie nipped at Maxie and pierced her ear. After that trauma, Maxie was submissive around Gracie. Her upright tail would tuck under her bottom. She would sink to the ground and lower her head. She would not look Gracie in the eye.

Maxie is a master of two responses to danger. Her natural response towards another dog is to fight. Not truly interested in hurting the other dog, she simply wants to let the other dog know that she is in charge.

On the occasion when the other dog beats her to the top of the pecking order, such as with a yapping terrier or Gracie, her response is flight. She walks the other way or stays in the car. She wants nothing to do with a dog whose bark warns of a big bite.

Like Maxie, we respond to danger with fight or flight. If verbally attacked, we might grow angry and feel our hackles rise. If the doctor gives us a poor diagnosis, we might climb the ramparts and say, "I'll do whatever it takes!" We resolve to be more prayerful, more patient, and more disciplined. We commit to try harder.

Or we might decide that, when faced with a relentless force, it is wiser to retreat. We hold our tongue, perhaps say, "I'm sorry," and move on as fast as possible. As if in a game of cards, we fold our hand. We accept the state of affairs as it is and back down.

In situations where we are powerless, the normal response is fight or flight. I would like, however, to explore a third way.

THORNY OPPORTUNITY

Cathy had been a successful realtor. Before the housing market collapsed in 2008 into the basement, she had been the primary breadwinner. Bill worked odd jobs painting and doing handyman work during school hours that padded the pin money, but it fell squarely on her shoulders to provide for their family.

She worked long hours, weekends and evenings, showing homes. Winning the monthly sales awards so many times, she stopped putting the framed certificates on her office wall. At the same time, she was a team player. She helped out other realtors. She gave her time to organize her office to help with community events such as Relay for Life. Having been raised by a single mother, she knew what it meant to need others. She believed in giving back.

While she worked, her husband Bill raised the three kids. One was finishing college and had a serious boyfriend. Another was graduating from high school with community college plans; the caboose was in middle school. She loved those rare times when she could watch Ethan's soccer games. She was so proud of her children.

Although their family looked like the American Dream, the marriage had deteriorated to "just friends." She loved Bill, but she was not in love with him. The years had gone into work and kids, and their marriage had grown apart. The only thing they talked about were the children. She found herself, as she considered herself in the bathroom mirror, wondering what a former high school boyfriend might be up to these days.

The financial stress widened the cracks. Her mother's house, which she had sworn she would take care of, had been lost in foreclosure when she could no longer pay the mortgage. Their own house mortgage was so deep underwater that she could not imagine ever catching up. They had lost their rental properties and their boat and jet skis. Every time she opened a closet and saw toys, tools, clothes, and shoes rarely used and long forgotten, she felt angry. Her hard work had bought grist for a yard sale.

Cathy lost sleep. Four o'clock in the morning seemed to be the favorite time for the anxieties to crawl out from under her bed to taunt her. Her head had been replaced by a permanent migraine. Bill slept the sleep of the innocent. It was not fair. Cathy despaired over her marriage and future.

Cathy had several choices. Rallying her energy, calling a marriage counselor, working harder and saving more, she could fight for her marriage and her family's future. Or, she could accept the status quo and the lax attitude of Bill, slowly letting their financial black hole swallow them. Or, she could try a third way.

Neither fight nor flight, the third way was to seize her moments of despair as opportunities for prayer. For example, when Cathy opened a closet door and smoldered before self-absorbed spending, it was an opportunity to pray.

"Lord, I can't stand looking at this. I am burning up with anger over my family's waste. We've made a real mess of things. Only you can make something good come out of this situation. So I give to you this closet, this house, and my family." In a few short words, the blaze of anger was redirected to say, "I can't. You can. I'm yours."

The resentments that Cathy felt towards her husband Bill were opportunities for prayer. Instead of stewing through the darkest hours of the night, she could instead take a deep breath and make a nighttime prayer.

"Lord, it's me again. Just like last night, I'm wide awake in the dark, angry. Even though it's not fair, even though it does not make sense, I have to do what Jesus said and forgive. So, please, bless Bill. Give him a good night's rest. Let him wake up refreshed. Help him to know your love for him. Renew between us our respect and love."

Forgiving comes more easily when you own up to your proper share of the situation. A good examination of conscience takes responsibility for your own actions and softens the bitter heart. This is not to excuse bad behavior, let alone give free rein to actions destructive to a marriage and family. But taking the opportunity to pray for a person you are having difficulty with replaces the blame-game with love. It brings the saving power of the cross into the impossible situation which causes you to despair.

When you say those six words, look at what happens to those times of crisis. The occasions of fight or flight become opportunities for a quick prayer. Inviting God's grace into the moment, you no longer rely on your power to make things better. You can face the moment as it is.

For instance, when an attractive person walks into the gym while you are working out, you might take flight and look away at anything but that person, pretending not to stare at him or her. Or, you might fight the desire to lust and tell yourself, "I'm better than that. I won't look again." Either way, flight or fight, you likely find yourself stealing glances and battling distracted thoughts.

There is the third way. You can simply invite the Lord into the situation and pray, "I can't deal with my desire. Only you, Lord, can. Bless them. Give them a good day." Bringing the Lord into the moment changes everything. It is no longer up to you to fight or take flight. You have a new way. The moment of crisis becomes an opportunity to pray.

The six words "I can't. You can. I'm yours," free you to say three more words, "I don't know." Having admitted to yourself and God that you are overwhelmed and powerless, it is easier to tell others that you don't know what to do. You may know some things and have some ideas, but now you can accept that it is not completely up to you to figure out what to do.

You can even go further than saying, "I don't know," and add three words guaranteed to stop an argument dead in its tracks: "You are right."These three words will produce more peace than a month of counseling. Having surrendered the notion of telling God what to do, it is easier to let go of the need to tell others what to do. Whether you are right or wrong takes a backseat to the powerful consolation that you belong to the Lord.

Saint Paul wrote in his second letter to the Corinthians that he was given a thorn in his flesh. Many have speculated exactly what the thorn was. Some think that it was an infirmity or perhaps temptations of the flesh. It could have been the short fuse on his temper. It could have been an obnoxious opponent or faction. Like a thorn, though, it was always present, an annoyance that he was powerless to remove. Paul said that it was like a slap in the face, a rebuke that hurt his pride.

Three times Paul prayed to the Lord to take it away. Three times Paul begged the Lord to remove this thorn. Paul had given his life to preach the Gospel. He had left his homeland and traveled the known world to start communities of faith. He faced great persecution and eventually gave his life for the faith. Surely the Lord would hear Paul's plea.

What, then, did the Lord do when Paul begged him to remove the thorn in his flesh? What did the Lord do for his faithful servant? Nothing! The Lord told Paul, "My grace is enough for you; my great strength is revealed in weakness." In other words, the Lord used Paul's weakness to show his own strength. What was a thorn to Paul was an opportunity for the Lord.

Paul made his peace. No longer desperate to be rid of his thorn, he boasted in it. His change of heart was not a "grin and bear it" acceptance. He realized, "Whenever I am weak, then I am strong" (2 Corinthians 12:9-10). His weaknesses, having driven him to rely on the Lord's strength, became the source of his strength.

In addition to this thorn, Paul rejoiced in his suffering, humiliations, and persecutions. For him, they were opportunities for the Lord to show his strength. Paul, weak and afflicted, could not have accomplished on his own all that he did. His success in spite of his sufferings was proof to skeptics that the Lord was working through him. His thorn was an opportunity not just for prayer. It was an opportunity to boast!

Taking Up the Cross

Paul called his suffering a thorn in the flesh. More commonly, we call our suffering a cross. Our suffering connects us to the cross of Jesus Christ.

After Jesus was arrested by the authorities and interrogated by a religious court and then a political court, he was beaten and tortured to the edge of life. The 2004 film *The Passion of the Christ* graphically presented his torture. Blood from his flogging spattered on the sandals of the Roman soldiers. As they dragged off his bloody body, a long red streak followed. His mother Mary and Mary Magdalene, bent down on their hands and knees, soaked up with white cloths the blood puddled between the cobblestones.

Meanwhile, the soldiers who had whipped Jesus were not finished with him. They made a crown of thorns and pushed it into his skull using wood handles. Blood ran down his forehead. They forced Jesus to carry the heavy crossbeam through the crowded streets. Once he was at the site of his crucifixion, the soldiers pinned his hands. They drove spikes through his hands into the crossbeam. Blood dripped from the nail points to the earth.

As Jesus hung upon the cross, the authorities sneered at him, "He saved others. Why doesn't he save himself?" The soldiers jeered, "If you are the King of the Jews, save yourself." Even one of the thieves crucified next to Jesus mocked him. "What kind of savior are you? Can't you save yourself?" The crucified thief added, "And while you are at it, save me. Get me down from here!"

Jesus could have taken the easy way out and called on a legion of angels to protect him. After all, he was the Son of God. Unlike Adam and Eve, however, he was obedient to God the Father. Becoming fully human, he accepted the suffering of the human condition. He bore the consequence of sin. His death on the cross was the surrender that saves humanity.

Jesus was not the kind of savior who saved himself. He came to save others. He saved us through freely handing himself over to death on the cross. Although he could have escaped death, for our sake he freely chose it.

While crucified on the cross, he did not resign himself to his fate. His cross became the opportunity for his greatest act. In the gospel of Luke, he prayed for his persecutors. "Father, forgive them, for they do not know what they are doing."

His mission was to reconcile heaven and earth. Sent to take away the sin of the world through his own flesh, he made forgiveness the prayer from the cross. With his blood, he poured out his last words. He prayed for the forgiveness of those who had nailed him to the cross and mocked him.

In the gospels of Mark and Matthew, Jesus' prayer from the cross was not as peaceful as in the gospel of Luke. Jesus called upon God using the words of Psalm 22. "My God, why have you abandoned me?" Even in the midst of his greatest despair, he still claimed God as "my God."

In the gospel of John, Jesus prayed from the cross, "It is finished." His work of redemption was completed. He had overcome sin and death with his own death. Then he bowed his head and delivered his spirit.

As you bear your cross, you share in the redeeming cross of Jesus Christ. In the darkest times, you might say with him, "My God, why have you abandoned me?" At times when you have made your peace with the forces against you, you might pray with Jesus, "Father, forgive them, for they do not know what they are doing." And when your suffering becomes redemption for you and others, you can say with Jesus, "It is finished."

Saint Paul boasted in his cross. To him, his suffering for the sake of the Gospel was the source of his strength. When he was weak, the Lord was strong. This is not to minimize the cross; just the opposite. It is to take up the cross and carry it with the Lord.

OFFER IT UP

One morning I visited the children's hospital. Brian was recovering in the intensive care unit. He had had heart surgery to replace a defective valve. He had had a less complicated but similar surgery when he was an infant, and they knew this day would come when he would need the surgery again.

The surgery was not a final cure. They expected he would need the same surgery in ten or fifteen years. It was a serious condition he lived with. His summer was for recovery from the surgery so that he would be ready for school in August.

Brian was sitting up in a hospital reclining chair. He looked tired but okay. His mother pulled up another chair for me.

I asked, "Brian, how is your mother doing?" His mother had been with him for four days. She had not left his side even to take a shower. Her sister was in town for the week to help her husband with the three other children at home.

He said, "She's good."

I wondered aloud, "Have you ever heard the phrase, 'Offer it up'?"

"Sure," he said. "You offer your suffering to God for someone else."

He had nailed it. I was surprised. "How did you know that?"

"My mom," he said. "She taught me."

I imagined that she did more than her share of offering it up. "Who do you offer it up for?"

"My brothers and my aunt," he said without missing a beat. He had two older brothers and one younger brother. Offering up his suffering, he let it mean something for them.

Through our conversation, Brian's mother simply listened as though it was a perfectly normal conversation to have with a boy whose fourteenth birthday was in a few weeks. It turned out that, prior to surgery, Brian and his mother had talked about offering his suffering from the surgery and recovery for his aunt who had been recently diagnosed with breast cancer.

I asked them if there was anything they wanted to pray for in particular. Brian wanted to pray for the other sick people. His mother wanted to pray for his recovery and return home. I added prayers for the nurses and doctors and aides who took care of them.

We prayed together, "Our Father, who art in heaven,…."

I offered them communion, saying, "Behold, the Lamb of God who takes away the sins of the world. Blessed are those who are called to the supper of the Lamb," and gave them the Body of Christ.

After a few moments of quiet, I gave them a final blessing and hug goodbye.

Leaving Brian and his mother at the hospital, I drove to a rehabilitation facility. A parishioner had asked me to visit a friend, Nathaniel, who was not Catholic and attended a Protestant church.

Nathaniel had been on a motorcycle ride from Sanford to the beach simply for the joy of a sunny Sunday afternoon. Cruising at the speed limit, he did not have a chance when a car pulled onto the highway in front of him.

His motorcycle hit the car. Nathaniel flew. Finding himself on his back unable to move, he heard two people say, "Did you see how far he went?" A helicopter lifted

Nathaniel to the Orlando hospital where the doctors struggled to save his life. Amazingly, he could still wiggle his toes and fingers. His helmet had protected his head. But both his legs were broken. His pelvis had shattered like an egg. If he survived, he would be in rehab for a long time.

After listening to Nathaniel bring me up to date on his crash and injuries, I took a stab. "Have you ever heard the phrase, 'Offer it up?'"

"No," he said. "What's that?"

"It's joining your suffering with the suffering of Christ on the cross." He looked at me. "Just as Christ's sufferings on the cross save the world, your suffering can help others."

I didn't have my Bible with me. But if I did, I would have told Nathaniel that Saint Paul himself taught us to offer it up.

"Now I rejoice in my sufferings for your sake, and in my flesh I am filling up what is lacking in the afflictions of Christ on behalf of his body, which is the church" (Colossians 1:24).

In the course of his journeys throughout Greece and Asia Minor to tell people about Jesus Christ, Paul suffered greatly. He was persecuted, put in prison, beaten and tortured numerous times. He was run out of town. He was shipwrecked and nearly drowned. As mentioned earlier, Paul suffered a constant thorn in his flesh.

Saint Paul did not just put up with his sufferings. He took joy in them. While a masochist perversely delights in his own sufferings, Paul did not suffer for suffering's own sake. Paul rejoiced in his sufferings for others. More than a selfless act on behalf of others, Paul saw his suffering as filling up "what is lacking" in Christ's sacrifice.

You might wonder about his claim to fill up "what is lacking" in the afflictions of Christ. Was Paul saying that the passion and death of Jesus Christ were not enough to save us? Of course not.

Consider Simon of Cyrene. He was happening by when Roman soldiers grabbed him. The soldiers had a problem. They were force-marching Jesus to his crucifixion. Jesus, however, was too weak from the torture and scourging and beating to carry his own cross to the crucifixion site.

The soldiers laid the cross of Jesus on Simon. Hardly a willing helper, he nonetheless carried the cross of Jesus to Calvary (Luke 23:26). He helped complete the passion and death of Jesus Christ.

We are like Simon of Cyrene. We are members of the Body of Christ. Just as we help Jesus when we tell people about God's love for them and serve people in his name, we can also carry his cross with him. Our sufferings, while not something we might have sought out, can become part of his sacrifice that saves the world. The big theological word for this is Redemptive Suffering.

Your sufferings take on new meaning when you "offer it up." Catch a finger in a door? Offer it up. Aching in your back at the end of the day? Offer it up. Grumpy from the baby interrupting your sleep three times last night? Offer it up. Does your boss make your workday a chaotic hell? Offer it up. Knock over a cup of coffee? Offer it up. Get trapped in a slow line at the grocery behind someone having a loud cell phone conversation? Offer it up.

The ten-hour car trip with restless kids to vacation with in-laws you can offer up for a friend struggling with their teenagers. The latest skin cancer procedure you can offer up for a co-worker going through a tough time. Hungry from a skipped lunch you can offer up for the hungry children in South Sudan.

Be warned. Offering it up is not as easy as it sounds.

A part of you might prefer to wallow in self-pity and say, "Poor me!" Feeling bad, you might take some consolation letting others know how miserable you are.

Another part of you might be in the habit to use your suffering to justify resentment. Your anger at the perceived unfairness of your situation can make you bully others and get your way. Giving up this power is difficult.

To offer up your pain and suffering, you need to make an intention ahead of time. It helps to have spent some time in prayer thinking about these things so that you can deal with your suffering in a new way and offer it up when the suffering comes along.

While teaching a summer session of preaching at Saint Meinrad Seminary in Indiana, my Monday intention was for the permanent deacon candidates I was teaching. My Tuesday intention was for the monks of Saint Meinrad. My Wednesday intention was for my classmates from my seminary days. My Thursday intention was for a parish search committee meeting on Thursday evening to discuss an open position. My Friday intention was for my family. Each day, a new intention presented itself.

You might start each day with a particular intention. Your day's catch-all intention might be for the souls in purgatory, a relative looking for a job, or a friend with a chronic illness.

Your intention can be respect for life from conception to natural death, the strengthening of marriages as the foundation of our society, care for planet earth our common home, or the intentions of the Pope. Or you can simply give it to God to use as he will. The petty annoyances and heavy crosses that the day might bring become opportunities to pray for an intention.

You can pray, "Lord, by your holy cross you have redeemed the world. Accept my offering for the sake of (fill in the blank). Unite it with your cross for the salvation of the world. Amen."

"Offer it up" is not just something you can do with your own crosses. You can suggest "Offer it up" to others. In the same way that I had prayed with Brian in the hospital and Nathaniel in rehab, you can give others this great gift. It makes their suffering more meaningful and less insufferable. Through the cross of Christ, it redeems them.

Mind you, saying to someone, "Offer it up," is not a way to duck your duty to care for one another. By no means is "offer it up" an excuse to do nothing.

When a paralyzed man was placed before Jesus, he did not say to the man, "Offer it up!" Jesus said, "Child, your sins are forgiven.... Rise, pick up your mat, and go home." And to everyone's amazement, the paralyzed man picked up his mat and went home (Mark 2:1-12).

Coming across a man with a withered hand, Jesus did not say, "Offer it up." Jesus said to the man, "Stretch out your hand." He stretched it out and his hand was restored (Mark 3:1-6).

When a violent storm swamped the boat and the disciples prepared for the worst, Jesus did not counsel them, "Offer it up." He rebuked the wind and said to the sea, "Quiet! Be still!" The wind ceased and there was great calm (Mark 4:36-41).

Jesus healed the sick. Often at cost to himself, he cured the leper, gave sight to the blind, and even raised the dead. In no way was his ministry limited to a glib, "Offer it up."

He expects no less of us who are the hands and feet of the Body of Christ. Jesus' story of the Last Judgment promises that when the Son of Man comes in his glory, he will separate the sheep from the goats with these words. "For I was hungry and you gave me food, I was thirsty and you gave me drink, a stranger and you welcomed me, naked and you clothed me, ill and you cared for me, in prison and you visited me" (Matthew 25:31-46). We are to do everything necessary and possible to care for the least and the last.

"Offer it up" becomes a means of our sanctification. Christ pours out the Holy Spirit among his Church to associate us "to his self-offering to his Father and to his intercession for the whole world" (*Catechism*, paragraph 739). We pray in the Mass immediately after the consecration of the bread and wine into the Body and Blood of Christ, "May he make of us an eternal offering to you." When we offer up our sufferings, we offer ourselves in Christ to God. Our joys and sorrows, our grief and hope, offered up in Christ give us a share in the inheritance of the saints.

WHEN GOD SEEMS ABSENT, INVITE JESUS IN

"And I tell you, ask and you will receive; seek and you will find; knock and the door will be opened to you" (Luke 11:9). This scripture verse captures how we might see ourselves before God. We knock again and again with hat in hand until the door opens.

Sometimes, though, it is the other way around. Jesus is knocking on our door! Let me tell you what I mean.

A woman kept losing her patience from taking care of her mother with early Alzheimer's disease. On top of getting two children ready for school each day and working part time outside the home, she was doing everything superhumanly possible to keep her mother living at home with them.

Occasionally, her mother asked the same question over and over, "When are the children coming home?"

The daughter answered, "In the afternoon, mom."

Five minutes later, the mother asked, "When are the children coming home?"

"In the afternoon."

Through the morning, the daughter patiently answered her mother's relentless inquiry, "When are the children coming home?"

After the hundredth time, she snapped, "I've told you. IN THE AFTERNOON."

The next day, it would start all over again. It was particularly hard when she had been up most of the night with her mother.

After the woman explained her situation, I asked her to picture her frustration. Although it was the last place she wanted to be, she sat still with eyes closed and noticed her impatience, anger at herself, misery, and guilt.

A few minutes later, I asked her, "Invite Jesus to be with you. Invite Jesus into whatever is going on. Don't ask him to take it away. Don't ask him to fix it. Just invite Jesus in and notice together your frustration."

She closed her eyes for a minute in silence. I prayed with her quietly.

"What did you notice?" I asked.

She replied that she felt peace. She felt a presence. The misery was still miserable, but she knew that she was no longer alone. She had hope.

The prayer exercise had shifted the focus. Instead of rushing from frustration to fixing, she noticed Jesus and his friendship. Jesus was knocking on the door. The woman only had to invite Jesus in.

Maz Kanata, in the *Star Wars* movie *The Force Awakens*, said, "The Force, it's calling to you. Just let it in."

The *Star Wars* writers "borrowed" this line from the Catholic church. We have been saying for two thousand years, "The Lord is calling to you. Just let him in."

Let me offer two more examples of what happened when someone invited the Lord Jesus in.

A young couple had been in a terrible car accident. They had accidentally killed a person who was crossing a busy road late at night in the rain. Although the couple was physically okay, they were devastated.

The young woman who had been driving the car could not sleep or eat. Even though the police said that she had not been at fault, she felt responsible for the life lost.

When asked to picture the scene at its worst, she saw the crash.

I said to her, "Say, 'Lord Jesus, be with me.' Don't say, 'help me' or 'fix it' or 'make me feel better'. Just say, 'Lord Jesus, be with me,' and notice what you notice."

Inviting the Lord into the scene, she remembered the kind policewoman who told her repeatedly, "It's not your fault. You did what you could." She remembered her phone call to her mother and her mother's words of comfort.

The Lord comforted the young woman through her mother and the police officer. He was with her through them. She found some peace.

In another example, a woman struggled with guilt and isolation. Although she was beautiful, she was an ice-queen. Her face expressed no emotion. Her voice was measured. Her entire manner was guarded.

Twenty years ago, she had had an abortion. She had buried her pain in her work. The long days at work had numbed her guilt and isolation. Her entire person had become emotionally and spiritually numb. While she had acquaintances, she had never married and had no friends.

When invited to picture her guilt and isolation, she closed her eyes and found herself alone in a dark room. The floor of the room was covered in garbage. She was surrounded by trash.

I asked her to take this picture to prayer and simply say, "Lord Jesus, be with me." For some minutes, she was quiet. She opened her eyes.

"What did you notice?"

"There was a knock on the door. I opened it. Jesus stood at the door smiling. He said, 'I can help you clean it up'."

Like a divine janitor, Jesus wanted to be with her in her mess. He did not judge her. He did not condemn her. He simply asked for permission to help clean things up.

The woman had a tear in her eye. She had a look of surprise. It was the first time I had seen her show any emotion.

Over the next few months, she became more involved in the church. She became friends with some widows who gave her unreserved mothering. She went on a retreat, joined a Bible study, and was soon a familiar and smiling face. She could laugh and love again.

You can pray in this manner. You can invite Jesus in. After some experience, you might invite others to follow these three steps:

1. Picture where you are at. You might be stressed out from Christmas activities such as visiting relatives, planning meals, and shopping. You might be grateful for the birth of your first granddaughter. You might be mourning the death of a loved one. You might be bored and distracted. Wherever you are, that's where

you start. Notice what's on your mind and what's on your heart. Maybe it feels like a weight on your heart. Maybe you picture yourself in a deep pit or floating on the ocean. Picture where you are at. Notice what you notice.

2. Invite Jesus in. Do not tell Jesus what to do. Do not ask him to fix the situation. Do not ask him for help or guidance. Simply pray, "Lord Jesus, be with me." Notice what you notice together.
3. Thank God for his mercy that saves us.

Scripture talks about the good news reaching to the ends of the earth. "He has remembered his mercy and faithfulness toward the house of Israel. All the ends of the earth have seen the victory of our God" (Psalm 98:3). The "ends of the earth" is not only geographical. It is spiritual. Christ comes to be with us in every place. He comes to be with us in our family and work, studies and play, sickness and health, worries and joys, and regrets and hopes.

The Lord is a gentleman. He rarely barges in. Instead, he tells us, "Behold, I stand at the door and knock. If anyone hears my voice and opens the door, [then] I will enter his house and dine with him, and he with me" (Revelation 3:20).

Pray where you are at. Invite him to enter with the words, "Lord Jesus, be with me." Let him in.

ONE LIGHT STILL SHINES

Marie had to tell her three children what had happened that morning. In her book, *One Light Still Shines*, she relates how she sat down on the sofa with Abigail, age 7, Bryce, age 5, and Carson, eighteen months. "I have something very sad to tell you." She cleared her throat and swallowed. "Today Daddy made some very bad choices, some people got hurt, some people died, and he died too."

Earlier that same morning of October 2, 2006, Charlie Roberts, the husband of Marie and father of their three children, went into an Amish schoolhouse in Lancaster County, Pennsylvania. Charlie took hostage ten Amish girls between the ages of seven and twelve years old. He sent home the boys, the schoolteacher, and her pregnant sister. Lining up the girls and binding their feet, he shot them one by one. Then he turned the gun on himself. Five of the Amish girls survived, and five died.

Although her three small children could not begin to understand what had happened, Marie huddled with them on the sofa and cried inside. "God, you have to fix this!"

Marie looked up through the open window. The sun shone warmly and a cool breeze blew. She felt these words whispered in her soul. "I am not going to fix it. I am going to redeem it."

Later that afternoon, Marie was sitting alone at the kitchen table when she saw five or six Amish men walking down the street. Black hats, black pants with suspenders strapped over their solid-color shirts, blue, gray, and green. Getting up and stepping toward the window, she hid behind the curtain. She panicked. They were coming to her house!

Running from the kitchen, she found her father in the backyard with her children. "Dad, a group of Amish men are coming down the street. What should we do?"

"It's okay, Marie," Dad said. "I'll go out and talk to them. You stay inside."

As Marie hid herself behind the kitchen window curtain, she watched the Amish men walk up the driveway. Her Dad came forward and met these long-time neighbors. One Amish man with a long gray beard opened his arms wide. Her father, shoulders heaving, fell into the comforting arms of his friend. The others offered embraces. Heads nodding, they spoke and listened before departing with handshakes and farewells.

Inside the house, her father told Marie and her waiting family, "They came out of concern for you, for the children, for all of us. They asked if you were okay, if the children were safe. They wanted to know what they could do for you. They asked how they could help."

He continued. "Every one of those men had a family member in the schoolhouse this morning. Can you believe they came to express concern for us? They wanted us all to know that they have forgiven Charlie and that forgiveness embraces us all. They spoke no words of anger, not the slightest hint of resentment, only assurance, concern, and comfort."

Later in the week, a representative of a local bank brought stuffed animal toys and cards from bank staff and customers for Marie's children. For Marie, the bank representative brought news that the bank had set up a trust fund for her children. Funded by donations, the trust fund took away the fear for the children's financial future.

That Saturday, there was the funeral for her husband, Charlie. As Marie and her family drove to the cemetery, a posse of reporters and photographers followed. Surprisingly, an Amish man met them at the cemetery. Another man appeared. An Amish woman in a black cape and bonnet followed. About three dozen Amish men and women formed a half circle across the road. After letting the hearse and car pass, they turned towards the grave. Protecting the family, they gave their backs to the cameras.

As they believe that it creates a graven image, the Amish do not let their pictures be taken. Yet they stood up for the wife and children of the man who had murdered their daughters. All of the parents of those ten Amish girls were in the group. Letting her know that she was not alone, they offered Marie words of consolation and compassion. She felt surrounded by light.

In those days after the Amish schoolhouse shooting, the shadow began to lift. Going beyond the cry to God,

"Fix it!", the Lord had a better plan. Out of the massacre, the Lord brought forth healing, restoration, and redemption to the community and her family.

With time, Marie began to live again, even to laugh and sing. To her amazement, she even married again. The light of God pierced her darkness and transformed the tragedy. She wrote her book to show that no matter how tragic life can be and no matter how dark it becomes, the light still shines.

For Discussion

- "In situations where we are powerless, the normal response is fight or flight." How was the Passion of Jesus neither fight nor flight? Where have you seen a way taken that was neither fight nor flight?

- Read 2 Corinthians 12:1-10. Saint Paul wrote in his second letter to the Corinthians that he was given a thorn in his flesh. Three times Paul begged the Lord to remove this thorn. What was a thorn in your flesh? What happened?

- "Offer it up" joins our suffering in prayer with the suffering of Christ on the cross. When did you "offer it up"? What blessing, if any, came through offering it up?

- "When God seems absent, invite Jesus in." Spend some time in this prayer exercise. First, picture where you are at. Next, invite Jesus in. Finally, thank God for his mercy that saves us. What did you notice?

Memory Verse

"Behold, I stand at the door and knock.
If anyone hears my voice and opens the door,
[then] I will enter his house and dine with him,
and he with me."
(Revelation 3:20)

Lord, Where You Will, There I Will Go

Lord, where You will, there I will go,
And what You will, let it be so.
Only Your will, help me to know.

Lord, when You will, the time is true
And when You will, willingly for You
today and always, I am, I do.

Lord, what You will, I gladly claim
And what You will, for me is gain;
It is enough that Yours I am.

Lord, because You will it, noble and fair,
and because You will it, I trust to dare.
My heart rests in Your hands, in Your care.

– *Blessed Rupert Mayer (author's translation)*

Herr, Wie Du Willst, So Will Ich Geh'n

Herr, wie Du willst, so will ich geh'n,
Und wie Du willst, soll mir gescheh'n.
Hilf Deinen Willen nur versteh'n.

Herr, wann Du willst, dann ist es Zeit,
Und wann Du willst, bin ich bereit.
Heut und in alle Ewigkeit.

Herr, was Du willst, das nehm' ich hin,
Und was Du willst, ist mir Gewinn.
Genug, dass ich Dein Eigen bin.

Herr, weil Du's willst, d'rum ist es gut,
Und weil Du's willst, d'rum hab' ich Mut.
Mein Herz in Deinen Händen ruht.

– *Blessed Rupert Mayer*

FIVE

Some Fruits of Prayer When You Need Hope

Mary was diagnosed in October with lung cancer. Deciding against chemotherapy and radiation that would give her at best a few more months in the hospital, she went home to spend her final weeks. She accepted that she was dying and used the time to prepare to meet the Lord.

Her children and grandchildren expected nothing less of her. How she faced her situation was how she lived. She endured a difficult marriage to her alcoholic husband, who died shortly after her son was born. Raising three children as a single mother, she returned to school to become a nurse. She sacrificed to send her children to Catholic school. Somehow she bore the death of her daughter who was only twenty-five years old in the prime of life.

Amazingly, she was not a bitter person. She loved being a grandmother. Her grandchildren remembered how she sang to them at bedtime. She taught them to swim and was the first in the lake. With all its ups and downs, she enjoyed life. She did not just survive; she thrived. How did she do this? The short answer, as given by Thomas Carlyle, is, "No pressure, no diamonds."

Consider that natural diamonds are formed under very high temperatures and pressures about ninety miles deep under the earth's surface. The diamonds travel to the surface when extremely rare deep volcanic eruptions tear pieces of the earth's mantle and deliver them quickly to the surface. It is not simply the "coal and pressure" we learned in grade school. But pressure is essential to form the diamond in the wedding band.

A common consolation in times of trouble is, "God does not give you more than you can handle." This comment is meant to reassure that God is in charge and things will work out. It also suggests that God gave us the trouble. This is not the case.

"God did not make death, nor does he rejoice in the destruction of the living" (Wisdom 1:13). These words from the Book of Wisdom in the Old Testament make clear that God does not want us to suffer nor die. Just the opposite! Jesus said, "I came so that they might have life and have it more abundantly" (John 10:10). God does not give us trouble to handle. He is not a big boss handing down crushing assignments. He is the Good Shepherd who laid down his life for his sheep.

Following the Good Shepherd does not protect us from trouble. Psalm Twenty-three makes clear that, even as the Lord is our shepherd, we still walk through the valley of darkness. The difference is that the Lord is at our side. "Even though I walk through the valley of the shadow of death, I will fear no evil, for you are with me; your rod and your staff comfort me" (Psalm 23:4). By his cross, he brings us through the valley of darkness to the Promised Land.[4]

What God does is transform the cross into the resurrection, darkness into light, sin into grace, slavery into freedom, death into life, and bread and wine into the

Body and Blood of Christ. The Lord does not take away the pressure. He uses it to transform coal into diamonds.

I would like to describe three of the diamonds that the Lord can form from the crushing darkness. As you pray "I can't. You can. I'm yours," you can expect to grow in humility, gratitude, and discipleship.

Humility

To see others walk an easy road to prosperity and good health while you are lying half-dead in the ditch can eat you up with envy. It is hard to be satisfied with the little you have when others have so much and do not even appreciate it. The envy extinguishes any spark of joy.

The antidote to envy is humility, along with goodwill and abandonment to the providence of God.[5] The prayer "I can't. You can. I'm yours," is a humble prayer. It acknowledges that you are powerless. It makes no demands on the power of God. Rather than rely on flattery or manipulation, it trusts the Lord to provide.

Joyce had recently become blind. A staff person of a government agency who was helping her live on her own took her to Wal-Mart. She had a list of items she had to buy.

"Can't do it," Joyce stiffened.

"Yes, you can," the staffer said. 'I'm right behind you."

Joyce swallowed her pride, went to customer service, and asked for help. They gave her a guide. They shopped together for toothpaste, shampoo, batteries, and a blouse.

At the check-out line, Joyce was relieved that she had made it. As she was taking the change from the cashier, the staffer stopped her. "How do you know what the cashier is giving you?"

Customers in the growing line watched. Joyce mumbled, "Please give me the money in order."

As she had been taught by the agency, she kept the one dollar bills flat. She folded the fives. She quartered the tens. She folded lengthwise the twenties.

The people in line caught on and volunteered, "Those are ones. Those are five dollar bills." Joyce put the folded bills into her wallet.

The people in line were not upset for having to wait longer. They knew she was taking a big step. They cheered Joyce.

Joyce was elated. When she asked for help, she could do it. "The one who humbles himself will be exalted" (Luke 14:11). She was thrilled.

Humility is the fruit of realizing that you are not the master of the universe. You give up the illusion that you only need rely on yourself. As you come to accept that God is the true master of the universe, you find it easier to give credit to the Lord.[6]

Praying "I can't. You can. I'm yours," frees you to be like Joyce. Setting aside your pride, you become more free to ask for help from the Lord and from others. To no one's surprise, the world does not end when you say, "I can't."

"Humility is the foundation of prayer," the *Catechism of the Catholic Church* teaches (paragraph 2559). Growing into the "I'm yours" in your relationship with the Lord depends on humility.

Adam and Eve, as I mentioned earlier, let themselves be deceived. They thought that they did not need the Lord. They wanted to replace God with themselves. Taking the fruit of the Tree of Knowledge of Good and Evil, they ignored God's command not to eat its fruit and chose instead to decide for themselves what was good and evil. In their pride, Adam and Eve put themselves first before God. Their lack of humility ruined their relationship with the Lord and cost them Paradise.

Humility is the path that restores your relationship with God. "Humble we must be, if to heaven we go, where the roof is high, and the gate is low," George Herbert penned. He might have had in mind the door to the Church of the Nativity in Bethlehem. The doorway stands less than five feet tall. To enter the church marking the humble birthplace of Jesus, you need to bow your head.

Some confuse humility with contempt for oneself. Humility is not humiliation. Consider that on the night before he died, Jesus took a towel and basin of water, kneeled on the stone floor and washed the feet of his disciples. Washing their feet was not an act of humiliation but a humble act of service.

A business consultant said that one mark of a humble leader is how he or she treats others. The humble leader treats everyone with respect, no matter the status or position. From an earlier era when the highest compliment was to be called a gentleman, the telling sign of a gentleman was how he treated those who could be of absolutely no use to him.

Although we are absolutely no use to him, God has treated us all with the greatest dignity. The Lord of all creation humbled himself to serve his servants. The Lord Most High became most low in order to raise us up. His humility made possible our salvation.

Humility is not thinking less of yourself but thinking of yourself less. By praying "I can't. You can. I'm yours," you become less selfish and more selfless. It is less about "me" and more about "thee." "Humble yourself the more, the greater you are," Sirach advises, "and you will find favor with God" (Sirach 3:17).

Gratitude

Thanksgiving Day was officially set as the fourth Thursday of November by President Abraham Lincoln. The Pilgrims had their feast in 1623, George Washington started this as a national holiday in 1789, but President Lincoln fixed the date we still use. And he did this when he did not have very much to be thankful about in his own life.

In October 1863, Lincoln's political future looked bleak. If he were defeated in the election of 1864, the Confederacy would gain its independence and the Union would be permanently split. His only real military victory to that point had been at Vicksburg. Many members of his own cabinet openly despised him and joked about him in public. Even his wife had been investigated as a possible traitor.

In the face of such personal and national crises, it would have made sense to call for a national day of prayer. He had already called for a national day of fasting in March 1863. But a national Day of Thanksgiving? At a time like that? What was Lincoln thinking?

President Lincoln must have discovered the same principle that Saint Paul lived by. At a low point in his life, Saint Paul wrote, "And be thankful. Let the word of Christ dwell in you richly ...with gratitude in your hearts to God" (Colossians 3:15-16). Paul was in prison, fully expecting to be executed, when he wrote those words. He was at odds with the local Christian community. And yet, like Lincoln, in the midst of great personal suffering, Paul counseled thanksgiving!

How could St. Paul from prison say, "Be thankful"? How could President Lincoln, in the darkest days of the Civil War, call for a national Day of Thanksgiving?

What they had learned was that in all circumstances, especially the worst, they needed to give thanks. They were not counseling, "Count your blessings," a code to distract from suffering and to escape to a happy place. They were not sighing, "Well, give thanks – it could be worse," and then feeling troubled about feeling bad. Giving thanks turned them to the goodness of God.

For the discipline of giving thanks, we have one more example. On the very night he was betrayed and entered into his Passion, Jesus shared the Passover meal with his disciples. "Then he took a cup, *gave thanks*, and gave it to them, saying, 'Drink from it, all of you, for this is my blood of the covenant, which will be shed on behalf of many for the forgiveness of sins'" (Matthew 26:27-28).

The Lord Jesus offered thanks to his Father for the very things that promised that he would be broken and poured out, flesh and bone, suffering beyond suffering. In giving thanks, he entered into his Passion, but not alone. He took with him the confidence of his Father's goodness. He took that faith to hell and back.

We celebrate the memorial of his death and resurrection every time we celebrate the Mass. In Christ, we offer the sacrifice of thanksgiving. The official word for the Mass itself, "Eucharist," is a Greek word that means "Thanksgiving." The Mass is one big thank-you to the Lord.

Giving thanks in good times and in bad, we enter into Christ's death and resurrection. God restores our confidence in his goodness, the goodness of life even at its worst. Just as St. Paul and President Lincoln lived and died by it, we live and die by the same rule of life.

Praying "I can't. You can. I'm yours," will make you more grateful. Instead of relying on your own strength and either succeeding or failing, instead of asking God to make things better and either they do or they do not improve, you renew your bond with God. "I'm yours" is not dependent on what you do or don't do. Nothing that happens to you can change God's love for you. Accepting his love is to accept a gift, and this makes you more grateful.

To grasp the gift of God held in the words, "I'm yours," we should explore three rules of gift-giving.

The first rule of gift-giving is that the person giving the gift must give the gift with no strings attached. For example, promising your children that you will take them to McDonald's for lunch if they behave is not a gift. It's a bribe. On the other hand, if you take your children to McDonald's just because you want to, that's a gift. Giving them a treat apart from their behavior is the difference between a reward and a gift. Giving without condition is the first rule of gift-giving.

The second rule of gift-giving is that the person who receives the gift must receive the gift as unconditioned. They must recognize that there are no strings attached.

On your birthday, for example, a co-worker surprises you. "Happy birthday! I'd like to take you out to lunch." You may find yourself forcing a smile while silently panicking, "Oh no! If I say yes, then I will have to take him out to lunch on his birthday!"

To your co-worker, the offer of lunch is a gift. There are no strings attached. To you, the offer of lunch implies a transaction. If you believe you must reciprocate, the lunch offer is not received as a gift. You might end up excusing yourself, "Thanks, but I have other plans," and hurrying the other way. For the gift to be a true gift, you do not have to do anything except accept or graciously decline the gift. It cannot be earned, deserved, or in any way returned.

The third rule of gift-giving is a paradox. The person receiving the gift must say, "Thank-you!" Yes, the second rule of gift-giving states that you are not obligated to do anything in return for the gift. All the same, you must acknowledge that the gift is a gift. Writing a thank-you note is not so much for the sake of the giver as it is for the receiver. It is a response of gratitude.[7]

Note that gratitude is not a feeling. You do not have to feel grateful for the pair of red and green socks that your fun-loving aunt gave you at Christmas. But you do have to say, "Thank you."

Gratitude is an attitude. It is the decision to see the gift as a gift. Giving thanks in writing or in words eventually fosters the feeling of gratitude. It takes practice. You become what you do. Giving thanks makes you a grateful person, able to appreciate your blessings and to feel blessed. Action leads to the attitude.

Give thanks to live in thanks. Give thanks with a smile and say, "Thank-you." Better still, write a note. (A hand-written note is more personal than a digital thanks.) One hospital ward had a sign on the exit door, "Thank you for allowing us to care for your loved one." Not only would the family of the patients understand the message, so would the nurses and doctors who worked on the floor. Their sign of thanks would remind them, on their way home after a long shift, that they had reason to give thanks.

An exercise to become more grateful towards God is to count your blessings. At the end of the day, simply name ten blessings you received that day. For example, you might say, "Thank you for a family dinner. Thank you for a cool evening. Thank you for a pleasant walk around the block. Thank you for shady oak trees," and so on.

The Human Performance Institute in Orlando coaches business leaders to maximize their energy and avoid burn-out. Business leaders from around the United States come to the seminars. One of the practices that the seminar advises is to keep a gratitude journal. Each evening, the CEOs are to write by hand, not typing or talking, what they are grateful for. Spending a few minutes at the end of the day writing a gratitude list seems too simple. Can this really be worth doing? Their very busy clients think so. If this is valuable advice for CEOs, why not try it?

The prayer, "I can't. You can. I'm yours," frees you from the notion that everything you have is the fruit of your hard work. It saves you from becoming bitter when things go from bad to worse despite your best efforts. It leads you to acknowledge that most things are beyond your power. You come to believe in God's desire and ability to give, with no strings attached, all that you need to love as God loves.

The proper response to a gift is to say thank-you. Let us give thanks to the Lord our God.

Discipleship

For every consoling verse of Scripture, you can find a verse that challenges. Jesus did not mince words. "Love your enemy! Do good to those who hate you!" are two of his hard sayings.

You may be battling a bureaucracy or besieged in a spiteful divorce. Where can you find the strength to love your enemy when it takes all that you have to get through the day?

One option is to read Scripture selectively. When battered by life, we naturally look for words that lift us up. We seek Scripture verses that comfort us and skip Scripture verses that confront us.

Marcion lived in the second century. He had difficulties with some of the Scriptures. His study of the Jewish Scriptures and the writings of the new Christian

Church led him to believe that the God of the Jewish Scriptures was irreconcilable with the teachings of Jesus. If read literally, the God of the Jewish Scriptures was not always just, good, or all knowing. Sometimes God was seen as crude and cruel.

To smooth the differences between the God of the Old Testament and the God of the New Testament, Marcion did away with Scriptures that were inconsistent with his idea of God. In his Bible, there was no Old Testament. He threw out the gospels of Matthew, Mark, and John. The Book of Revelation and the letters of Peter and John were omitted. His abridged Bible consisted of ten letters of Saint Paul and the Gospel of Luke.

Marcion's Bible was very popular. His Bible made so much more sense and eased inconsistencies between the books of the Bible. Even though the Church declared him a heretic, the church that he founded grew. For a century, it rivaled the Church.

The legacy of Marcion was that the Church began to distinguish more carefully which religious writings were from the apostolic tradition and which writings were not. Eventually the writings formed a canon, a list of officially approved religious writings, which became the New Testament that we have today.

The Church teaches that both the Old Testament and the New Testament reveal God to us. Excluding sections or focusing only on certain books of the Bible leads to a distorted understanding of God. While the various books and letters that make up the Bible can be confusing, they are a unity. Together they are the inspired and revealed word of God.

While you may not be as bold as Marcion to prune and publish your own version of the Bible, you likely have favorite Scripture verses and Bible stories. We naturally tend towards the texts that make us feel better. Who would not prefer comforting words over the hard sayings of Jesus?

With this six word prayer, "I can't. You can. I'm yours," you have another option. You no longer need to avoid hard sayings such as "Love your enemies." While powerless to love your enemies, you can openly and humbly come before the Lord. In your powerlessness, you must rely on him and build a strong foundation of faith with two words, "I'm yours." Facing honestly your inability to live the hard sayings in scripture, you can leapfrog those who live in the illusion that they are good if not perfect disciples.

Let's look at one challenging Scripture passage that you might normally skip in search of consolation. In the text, Jesus laid out the cost of discipleship in strong terms. "If anyone comes to me without hating his father and mother, wife and children, brothers and sisters, and even his own life, he cannot be my disciple. Whoever does not carry his own cross and come after me cannot be my disciple....Everyone of you who does not renounce all his possessions cannot be my disciple" (Luke 14:26-27, 33).

To those who have already been beaten down, his terms seem cruel. Is Jesus telling us to hate our family? Does he expect us to carry the cross to the bitter end? Does he really want us to give away everything we have?

His conditions of discipleship are impossible. The only possible response to his impossible demands is to pray as you would in any impossible situation. "I can't. You can. I'm yours." Let's break it down.

The first part of this hard saying on discipleship appears to hate the family. The saying about hating your father and mother and everyone else is a negative way to say, "Put God first." This commandment is the First Commandment. Until you get this right, you will struggle to keep all of the other commandments, including the Fourth Commandment, "Honor your mother and father." Honoring your mother and father is one of the great commandments. In the order of commandments, though, it takes fourth place to the First Commandment, "Put God First."

"Love God with all your heart, soul and strength," Jesus commanded (Mark 12:29-30). Put God before your wife and children, your siblings, and yourself. Do not let father, son, or brother come between you and the Lord. It is not a matter of putting down your love for your family. It is a matter of putting an even greater trust in God.

When you have a hard time loving yourself, this impossible command is the perfect time to pray. Your prayer may be something like, "Lord, I can't put you first. I can't imagine what you might ask of me if I put you before my family.

"But I believe that you can do all things. You can give me a greater trust in you. Your son Jesus said that whoever leaves his family behind will gain a hundred families more. He himself left you to come to us and make us your adopted children. So I am yours. I trust you with my family, my children, my life itself. Amen."

The second part of this hard saying on discipleship is about the cross. Jesus commanded his would-be disciples, "Take up your cross." The very things that we pray to be delivered from, Jesus demands us to embrace. He himself left behind the safety of his home in backwater Galilee. He traveled to Jerusalem, the city that cast out more than a few prophets. His whole purpose in life was to take up his cross. He was sent by God to die on the cross. In taking up his own cross, Jesus expected no less of his followers. "Take up your cross!"

The cross that is your daily burden is an impossible burden. You can shake your fist at God. "Why me? It's not fair!" After letting God know how unhappy you are, you can run away from your cross.

Or, you can pray. You can turn to the Lord and say, "I can't take up my cross. It is too heavy. When I can't bear it, I end up eating too much, smoking, or watching TV to dull the pain. I can't face my cross.

"Only you, Lord, can make this cross not just bearable. You can make it a blessing. I don't know how. I can't imagine it. But I believe that you can. You carried your cross for me. You are with me on my cross. I trust you to lead me on the way of this cross that I may share in your resurrection. I'm yours. Amen."

The third part of this hard saying on discipleship is about belongings. Jesus said that his followers must give up all possessions. "Everyone of you who does not renounce all his possessions cannot be my disciple."

This is not a misprint. In another passage in Luke chapter 18, he made perfectly clear his requirements when a rich official asked him, "What must I do to inherit eternal life?"

Jesus said, "Keep the commandments."

The rich official replied, "I've been keeping the commandments since I was a youth. Is that it?"

Jesus did not soften the demands of discipleship. "There is still one thing left for you: sell all that you have and distribute it to the poor, and you will have a treasure in heaven. Then come, follow me" (Luke 18:18-23).

Keeping the ten commandments was not enough. Going to Mass was not the one thing lacking. The command was clear. Sell everything, give it to the poor, and then follow Jesus.

The rich official became sad. Who could blame him? He was rich. Walk away from everything? Impossible![8]

The first option is to give up. We could dismiss Jesus' criteria for discipleship as hyperbole that only the saints take seriously. The second option is to try harder. We could take his command to heart and struggle to live a simple lifestyle. Either way, these two options rely on us. They depend on what we do. Either we give up or we try harder.

The third option is to take it to prayer. "Lord, I can't renounce everything. I don't have enough money as it is. How would I live? How would I take care of my family?

"You alone can free me from worry of having enough. You are the Good Shepherd who leads me to green pastures. You give me what I need for salvation. So ... I trust you with all that I have. I sign over to you my time, talent, and treasure. To remind me that all I have is a gift from you, I give to you a nickel of every dollar I earn. I'm yours. Amen."

Jesus had other impossible commands for his disciples. "Pray for those who persecute you" becomes a bridge too far when we are at the mercy of our boss. "Forgive seventy times seven times" sounds good in church but we wonder what Jesus would have said if he had met our extended family.

Jesus did not water down his discipleship requirements to a generic "Be good and avoid evil." No wonder budding disciples decided to turn around and go home.

Here is the good news: You do not have to water down the Gospel because you are in a lousy situation. Just the opposite. You can take on the full challenge of the Gospel because you are in a lousy situation. Those who are weak learn this more quickly than those who are strong. Instead of throwing in the bad hand dealt by life, you can more readily turn to the Lord Jesus Christ to play it for you.

Here's why: Nothing is impossible for God. I believe that Jesus gave us impossible commands, such as "Pray for those who persecute you," precisely so that we would rely on him and turn to him in expectant trust. Putting God first, carrying our cross, and renouncing possessions are impossible on our own. Jesus said, "What is impossible for human beings is possible for God" (Luke 18:27). With God, nothing is impossible.[9]

The prayer "I can't. You can. I'm yours," is a prayer to become a true disciple.

For Discussion

- "The Lord can form diamonds from the crushing darkness." When have you seen diamonds come from a crushing darkness?
- "Joyce was elated. When she asked for help, she could do it." When you asked for help, what happened?
- "The official word for the Mass itself, 'Eucharist,' is a Greek word that means 'Thanksgiving. The Mass is one big thank-you to the Lord." Count during a Mass how many times the prayers say "give thanks" or "thanksgiving."
- What is your cross? How has it made you a more faithful disciple?

Memory Verse

"What is impossible for human beings
is possible for God."
(Luke 18:27)

Breathe on Me, Breath of God

Breathe on me, Breath of God,
fill me with life anew,
that I may love what thou dost love,
and do what thou wouldst do.

Breathe on me, Breath of God,
until my heart is pure,
until with thee I will one will,
to do and to endure.

Breathe on me, Breath of God,
till I am wholly thine,
till all this earthly part of me
glows with thy fire divine.

Breathe on me, Breath of God,
so shall I never die,
but live with thee the perfect life
of thine eternity.

– Edwin Hatch, 1835-1889

Conclusion

Throughout this reflection on the prayer, "I can't. You can. I'm yours," we have seen that the prayer changes crises into opportunities to lean on the Lord, yielding fruits such as humility, gratitude, and discipleship. We have been circling one word – hope. To conclude these thoughts, let me finish with a few words about hope.[10]

Hope Is a Will and a Way

The *Life of Pi* is a fictional story about a teenager who drifted for months in a lifeboat in the Pacific Ocean. The freighter with his family sank off the Philippines in a storm at night. Pi was alone in a lifeboat.

In the lifeboat's storage compartments Pi found bottles of water, crackers, and a survival kit. From the survival kit, Pi read a little red book called *How to Survive in a Lifeboat*. The little red book gave tips: Set a strict daily schedule. Do not drink salt water. Catch fish. Above all, do not lose hope.

His survival was complicated by an adult male Bengal tiger in the boat called Richard Parker. I won't tell you how Pi managed to keep himself and the tiger alive, except to say that Pi followed the advice of the little red book – do not lose hope.

Spoiler alert! Pi lived to tell the tale. He survived because of a combination of two things.

First, he had a will to live. He did not want to die. He wanted to live. And he wanted Richard Parker, the Bengal tiger, to live as well.

Second, he had a way to live. The way included bottled water, crackers, protection from the sun, catching fish, a strict daily schedule, and so on.

Pi lived because he did not lose hope. He had a will and he had a way. He had hope.

Hope is a will and a way.

A wish is different than hope. For example, you may want to win the lottery. You dream about what you would do with a windfall – retire, travel the world, help the poor. Dream all you want, but you do not have any hope of winning the lottery unless you buy a lottery ticket. You need both the desire to win and a ticket in your hand to have any chance of cashing in. A will without a way is just a wish.

The will is just as important as the way. In the beginning of the calendar year, you might sign up with the local gym. You fill out the application and pay your new member's fee. Your credit card is set up for the automatic withdrawal of the monthly fee. You pump up your ipod with music. You order a pair of the latest cross-trainer shoes and one of the hi-tech shirts that wick away the sweat. With your new workout look, you hit the gym.

The first week of January, you feel good. You are in the gym Monday, Wednesday, and Friday. Saturday, you sleep in. Sunday afternoon, you decide that time with the family is more important. Monday morning of Week Two, you cram in a short workout before work. You don't return to the gym until Saturday. The only reason you show up is because you promised to be on the pick-up basketball team. By the end of January, your resolve to exercise is in the same pile as your diets.

You have the music and the gear and the gym, but no drive. Without the will, you have no hope of getting fit. Hope is both a will and a way. A way without a will is a road untraveled. It gets you nowhere.

God has a will. God's will is to save us from sin and death. His will is to share his own life with us.

God has a way. God's way is Jesus Christ. "I am the way, the truth and the life" (John 14:6).

The difference between regular hope and Christian hope is this – it's not about our will and our way. It's about God's will and God's way. God's will and way give us reason to hope.[11]

These reflections on the prayer, "I can't. You can. I'm yours," have value if they have helped you to have Christian hope. Trusting in God's will and God's way is the source of hope.

Throughout these reflections I have used illustrations from the saints such as Saint Peter, Saint Paul, and Saint Ignatius. We have taken a look at Scripture, especially the foundational story of the exodus of the people from slavery in Egypt to their entrance into the Promised

Land. We have spent time with Isaiah who promised unconditional love from the Lord.

I would like to leave you with one more saint from Scripture. This saint was powerless and without hope yet instrumental to the salvation of the world. He could be the patron saint for the strong silent types who have lost hope. These last words are for all the Josephs.

Joseph was a provider and protector. At least, he tried to be. You may know how Joseph, far from home, did his best to provide for his wife Mary a decent place to give birth to her son, Jesus. His best was an embarrassment, a barn in Bethlehem. Some provider he was.

When King Herod began to massacre the innocents, Joseph, the protector, went into action. He packed up his little family in the dead of night and fled to the strange land of Egypt. Two years later, after Herod had died, Joseph moved his little family to Nazareth and started over.

Joseph did all of this AFTER his hopes had been crushed.

He had held the hope of an honorable marriage to Mary. Their marriage had been arranged by their mothers and confirmed by the fathers. It was a community matter known throughout the village. Then Mary was found to be pregnant. It was not his child.

When his hopes were trampled, he would have been within his rights to humiliate Mary and her family. Instead, Joseph chose to act with honor. He would divorce her quietly. He did not go public.

Throughout the entire life-and-death drama, Joseph let his actions speak for him. Joseph, in all the verses of Scripture, never said a word. Mary, his wife, had plenty to say in the Bible. Her relatives, Elizabeth and Zechariah, had their say. From Joseph, though, not a word. After the marriage setback, no doubt he became more silent. His hopes flattened, it was time to move on.

But that was not what Joseph did. Bethlehem, Egypt, Nazareth, protector and provider, he did all of this after his hopes were crushed. What changed? What happened?

Joseph went to bed. That very night the angel of the Lord appeared in a dream to Joseph. The angel told Joseph about God's dream.

"Joseph, son of David," the angel said, "do not be afraid to take Mary your wife into your home. She will bear a son and you are to name him Jesus, because he will save his people from their sins" (Matthew 1:20-21).

They say, "Home is where the heart is." Well, God's dream was to make his home with his people, where his heart is. When God heard his people cry out, not knowing which way to turn, God joined them. God's dream was to be with us so that we would be with him.

To make his dream come true, the Lord God needed a man of action. God wanted Joseph to be part of his dream to save the world.

If Joseph was to dream with God, he had two things to do.

First, let go. He had to let go of an honorable marriage to Mary and quietly accept dishonor. Every gossip in Nazareth, even the slowest, could count to nine. His reputation as a god-fearing man was ruined. He had to let go of a little Joey Junior and instead claim a child that wasn't his. He had to let die the ambition of a respectable life as a righteous provider and protector.

In short, Joseph had to let go his hope, his will and his way. His dreams were good dreams. There was nothing wrong with those dreams. Only, God was dreaming something more for Joseph.

Second, give God. In letting go his own hope and embracing God's hope, Joseph would have to change. He would still be a provider and protector. Only now Joseph would become the protector of the One who protects us from evil. Joseph would become the provider for the One who provides us all we need. He would have to give God his ability and put at the service of the Lord what he could do best – provide and protect.

Joseph woke up. He made up his mind. No words, just actions. Joseph simply got up and got Mary. Instead of moving on, he had Mary move in. Still silent, even in the face of wagging tongues, he followed God's dream. He named the child and claimed him as his own. God's will and way became his hope.

Bethlehem, Egypt, Nazareth, the cross. He did not know what the future held. Joseph only knew that the hope of the world was God's dream in Jesus the Christ.

To you Josephs who have no hope, go to bed. That's where new dreams are made.

But first, kneel at the side of your bed and say a prayer. Pray, "Lord, I've lost my will. I've lost my way. I don't have a back-up plan. Let your will be done for me and my family. Show me your will and your way. Show me how to provide for and protect, not just my family, but your dream for the world. Amen."

If you don't know what to say, just remember six words. "I can't. You can. I'm yours." And it would not hurt to add, "Saint Joseph, pray for me."

ACKNOWLEDGEMENTS

I would like to thank Bert Ghezzi for editing and encouragement, Linda Romigh, Dianne Kramer, and Tyler Band for corrections and grammar, Father Tom Connery for pastoral advice, Tim Schoenbachler for book layout and technical support, and my favorite older sister Theresa Degler for the cover design. I am grateful to the people I have served in six parishes. Marcia, Valerie, Cathy, and Mary (names and details have been changed) are only a few of the countless who have strengthened my faith, hope, and love. The Jesuits of Sacred Heart Retreat Center in Sedalia, Colorado, especially the late Dick Dunphy, S.J., have been a blessing. Finally, I owe a debt of gratitude to St. Peter, St. Paul, St. Ignatius, St. Maximilian Kolbe, Pope St. Paul VI, and St. Joseph who entrusted themselves to the Lord and inspire me to do the same.

Endnotes

[1] *Catechisms of the Catholic Church*, paragraph 1803 (CCC 1803). Some virtues are acquired by our effort, while some virtues are gifts from God. The cardinal virtues of prudence, justice, fortitude, and temperance are acquired by human effort with God's help in education, deliberate acts, and perseverance. The theological virtues of faith, hope, and charity are "infused by God into the souls of the faithful to make them capable of acting as his children and of meriting eternal life" (CCC 1813). They are God's gift to us that change our relationship with God as we cooperate with them. Finally, the seven gifts of the Holy Spirit are wisdom, understanding, counsel, fortitude, knowledge, piety, and fear of the Lord. They sustain the moral life. See "The Virtues" (CCC 1803-1845) in:
https://www.usccb.org/beliefs-and-teachings/what-we-believe/catechism/catechism-of-the-catholic-church
(retrieved September 7, 2020)

[2] Mark O'Keefe, *Virtues Abounding: St. Thomas Aquinas on the Cardinal and Related Virtues for Today* (Eugene, Oregon: Cascade Books 2019), 71. My description of temperance in eating, drinking, and sex rely on his insights, pages 78-82.

3 The full text of Saint Faustina's diary is at :
https://www.saint-faustina.org/diary-full-text/
(retrieved September 7, 2020)

[4] Pope Saint John Paul II reflected on the Christian meaning of human suffering in his apostolic letter, *Salvifici Doloris.* His key insight is that "suffering is present in the world in order to release love." It elicits the best in us to be like the Good Samaritan. It transforms "the whole of human civilization into a 'civilization of love'." See:
http://www.vatican.va/content/john-paul-ii/en/apost_letters/1984/documents/hf_jp-ii_apl_11021984_salvifici-doloris.html
(retrieved September 14, 2020)

For further thoughts about sufferings, see the chapter "What You Can Say About Suffering" in my book, *Can I Say A Prayer With You?*

[5] "Envy is sadness at the sight of another's goods and the immoderate desire to have them for oneself. It is a capital sin. The baptized person combats envy through good-will, humility, and abandonment to the providence of God" (CCC 2553-2554).

[6] For Aquinas, humility is a form of modesty that regulates our desire to attain, achieve, and excel. Humility tempers these desires with reality that we live in the truth of who we are, honestly appraising our real abilities and accomplishments. For example, we attribute humility to the athlete who achieves great feats yet recognizes the gifts and opportunities that made their accomplishments possible. In contrast, pride is the opposite of humility. Our desire to achieve becomes a vice when it is out of touch with reality and leads us to overly esteem our abilities and accomplishments and think of ourselves better than others. See O'Keefe, *Virtues Abounding*, pages 84-85.

[7] Aquinas considers the virtue of gratitude as a form of the cardinal virtue of justice. Like friendliness, generosity, and appropriate recompense, gratitude contributes to the health of our relationships and communities in its concern for favors done and gifts freely given. The sincere thanks and thank-you notes, while not required by justice, are appropriate ways to respond to a favor and nurtured by the virtue of gratitude. See O'Keefe, *Virtues Abounding*, pages 39-40.

[8] In the original saying in the gospel of Mark 10:17-22, the rich man went away sad. In Luke's version, the story ends differently. "But when he heard this he became quite sad, for he was very rich." It does not say that he went away. As in the story of the prodigal son where the final scene of the father and the older son lacks resolution and leaves us like the older son to decide whether to resent

or rejoice, perhaps Luke is leaving the ending open for us to decide whether we will leave or follow.

[9] See the story of Jesus in the garden of Gethsemane entering into his Passion. Faced with an impossible path, he prayed, "Abba, Father, all things are possible to you. Take this cup away from me, but not what I will but what you will" (Mark 14:36).

[10] Deeper theological reflection on Christian hope is beyond the scope of this little book. A surprisingly readable and inspiring reflection on Christian hope is the 2007 encyclical letter "On Christian Hope" (*Spes Salvi*) by Pope Benedict XVI. He recognizes that we have "little hopes" such as the love of family and friends, the attainment of position in a profession, the anticipation of a vacation or a family celebration, the satisfaction of work well done, the blessing of good health, and so on. "When these hopes are fulfilled, however, it becomes clear that they were not, in reality, the whole. It becomes evident that man has need of a hope that goes further" (paragraph 30). In search of that further hope, our contemporary age has put its hopes in scientific knowledge and scientifically based politics to create a perfect world. This hope in progress, however, is constantly receding. Our hopes keep us going day by day, but what gives them meaning is the underlying "great hope." "This great hope can only be God, who encompasses the whole of reality and who can bestow upon us what we, by ourselves, cannot attain. The fact that it comes to us as a gift is actually part of hope. God is the foundation of hope: not any god, but the God who has a human face and who has loved us to the end, each one of us and humanity in its entirety. His Kingdom is not an imaginary hereafter, situated in a future that will never arrive; his Kingdom is present wherever he is loved and wherever his love reaches us. His love alone gives us the possibility of soberly persevering day by day, without ceasing to be spurred on by hope, in a world which by its very nature is imperfect. His love is at the same time our guarantee of the existence of what we only vaguely sense and which

nevertheless, in our deepest self, we await: a life that is "truly" life" (paragraph 31). Christian hope is the hope for life beyond death, the thirst for ultimate truth, goodness, beauty, and peace, the hope for communion with God himself. See:

http://www.vatican.va/content/benedict-xvi/en/encyclicals/documents/hf_ben-xvi_enc_20071130_spe-salvi.html
(retrieved September 29, 2020)

[11] In the Mass immediately following the Lord's Prayer, the priest prays, "Deliver us Lord, we pray, from every evil, graciously grant peace in our days, that by the help of your mercy, we may be always free from sin and safe from all distress, *as we await the blessed hope and the coming of our Savior, Jesus Christ*" [emphasis added]. The ground of our hope is the coming of the Lord Jesus Christ. His death and resurrection anticipate the coming reign of God when all creation and humanity will be fully reconciled to God and in communion with him.

www.ingramcontent.com/pod-product-compliance
Lightning Source LLC
LaVergne TN
LVHW091055150826
845673LV00002B/591

* 9 7 9 8 5 9 0 6 0 4 0 9 8 *